GOD LAND

Reflections on
Religion and Nationalism

The William E. Massey Sr.
Lectures in the History of
American Civilization

1987

I fear that . . . God Land will be . . .
as great a God with us English
as God Gold was with the Spaniards

— Roger Williams, 1664

❑ GOD LAND

Reflections on Religion and Nationalism

Conor Cruise O'Brien

Harvard University Press
Cambridge, Massachusetts
London, England   1988

Copyright © 1988 by the President and Fellows of Harvard College
All rights reserved
Printed in the United States of America
10 9 8 7 6 5 4 3 2 1

This book is printed on acid-free paper, and its binding materials
have been chosen for strength and durability.

Library of Congress Cataloging-in-Publication Data

O'Brien, Conor Cruise
  God land : reflections on religion and nationalism /
  Conor Cruise O'Brien.
     p.   cm.—(The William E. Massey Sr. lectures
  in the history of American civilization)
  Bibliography: p.
  Includes index.
  ISBN 0-674-35510-5 (alk. paper)
  1. Nationalism—Religious aspects.   I. Title.   II. Series.
BL65.N3037 1988   87-32168
320.5′4—dc19   CIP

for Alan Heimert

Acknowledgments

I am grateful to Professor Stephan Thernstrom and the members of the committee responsible for the William E. Massey Sr. Lectures in the History of American Civilization for inviting me to deliver these lectures at Harvard in March 1987; to the members of the Harvard faculty who took the chair at individual lectures—Stephan Thernstrom on two occasions, my friend and fellow countryman Seamus Heaney, and my friend George Abbott White; and also to the Harvard audiences, some of whose questions opened up new lines of inquiry and influenced the revision of the lectures into the present book. I am grateful also to Harvard University Press, and in particular to Aida D. Donald and Ann Louise C. McLaughlin for editing the text for publication and for a number of valuable criticisms and suggestions.

Over the past five years I have been exploring various aspects of religion and nationalism in lectures at several other American universities. The Massey Lectures are the fullest expression to date of the results of that inquiry. As these lectures would not have assumed their present form without questions and comments at the other universities in question, it is fitting that I should also give thanks to Allan Bloom and the John M. Olin Center for the Study of Democratic Institutions at the University of Chicago; Marysa Navarro and colleagues at Dartmouth College; Susan Dunn and Mark Taylor at Williams College; Vivian Mercier and colleagues at the University of California at Santa Barbara; Thomas Flanagan and colleagues at the State University of New York at Stony Brook; and to the following nine students, all of whom made valuable contributions to my 1987 seminar on Religion and Nationalism in the Department of History at Williams College: Andrew P. N. Erdmann, Steven H. Fagin, Anne Gilbert, Michael Hunter, Nicholas Levis, David Reiss, Daniel M. Richmond, Stephen Theodore, and Stewart G. Weaver.

Howth Summit
Dublin, Ireland

Contents

GOD LAND

Reflections on
Religion and Nationalism

□ 1

Chosen Peoples, Promised Lands

The word "nationalism" is not to be found in the Hebrew Bible. But then, the word "religion" is not to be found in the Hebrew Bible either. Yet the forces to which we apply these words permeate the Bible and interact with one another.

Some people may have doubts about a part of that. Hardly the part about religion. Few people, whether religious or not, would deny that religion is to be found in the Hebrew Bible, even if the word for it is not there. But many people would deny that nationalism is in the Bible. Nationalism is a very modern word, and is often assumed to be a very modern thing.

There seems to be some confusion here, arising from the fact that the word nationalism is used in two different senses, each referring to a distinct set of phenomena. Yet the difference and the distinction are often ignored, even in textbooks on the subject.

The two senses are: nationalism as doctrine or ideology; and nationalism as a collective emotional force. In this second sense—that in which it is most frequently and widely used—the word is invariably preceded by a national adjective: German nationalism, Arab nationalism, Italian nationalism, Polish nationalism, and so on.

A good example of the prevailing confusion between these two concepts can be found in the entry under "nationalism" in a recent encyclopedia of political thought. The article starts out by asserting that nationalism is "by far the most potent ideology in the world." Now nationalism-as-ideology is not in fact particularly potent in the world today. Nationalism-as-ideology is altogether eclipsed, in its intellectual development, in its acknowledged influence over states, and in the number of its doctrinal adherents by an *internationalist* and *antinationalist* ideology: Marxism-Leninism.

What is powerful is not nationalism-as-ideology, but the other sort: the type that always carries a prefix and an emotional charge.

The area in which the power of nonideological nationalism has been most strikingly demonstrated in the second half of the twentieth century is precisely the area dominated by the internationalist and antinationalist ideology of Marxism-Leninism. Chinese Marxists broke away from Russian Marxists, Vietnamese Marxists from Chinese Marxists, Cambodian Marxists from Vietnamese Marxists. None of these attempted to justify their breaking away in terms of nationalist ideology. On the contrary, they continued, after the breach as before, to profess the internationalist and antinationalist ideology of Marxism-Leninism. But the breaches were all along national lines, and they were clearly prompted by nationalist feelings, including the feeling of not wanting to be instructed by foreigners, even in what concerned a commonly accepted internationalist ideology. Similar processes, with modifications, have been observed in Europe, in Albania, Yugoslavia, Romania, Italy.

The modern ideology of nationalism is about two centuries old. It rises almost simultaneously in the intellectual life of two great rival nations, France and Germany. Cultural nationalism as ideology begins in Germany with Herder; post-Christian political nationalism begins in France with Rousseau. I shall say more later about Herder's nationalism and Rousseau's, and their complex relations with religion.

Nationalism, as a collective emotional force in our culture, makes its first appearance, with explosive impact, in the Hebrew Bible. And nationalism, at this stage, is altogether indistinguishable from religion; the two are one and the same thing. God chose a particular people and promised them a particular land.

Let me briefly recall the main land-promises. God says to Abraham: "Lift up now thine eyes, and look from the place where thou art northward, and southward, and eastward, and westward: For all the land which thou seest, to thee will I give it, and to thy seed for ever" (Gen. 13:14–15). Again to Abraham, God specifies the limits of the Promised Land: "Unto thy seed have I given this land, from the river of Egypt unto the great river, the river Euphrates" (Gen. 15:18).

I'm sorry if this is beginning to sound a bit like a sermon, but these texts are basic to the subject matter of this book.

Again to Abraham, God says: "And I will give unto thee, and to thy seed after thee, the land wherein thou art a stranger, all the land of Canaan, for an everlasting possession; and I will be their God" (Gen. 17:8).

The promise is repeated, in slightly varying forms, to Isaac (Gen. 26:1–5) and to Jacob (Gen. 28:1–5; Gen. 35:11–12). And it is made to the Israelites collectively: "And I have also established my covenant with them, to give them the land of Canaan, the land of their pilgrimage, wherein they were strangers" (Exod. 6:4).

Now Christianity—the Christianity of Jesus and Paul and the early Christians—turns away from this whole conception of any earthly Promised Land. They didn't expect there to *be* any land, for much longer. Jesus said to Pilate: "My kingdom is not of this world" (John 18:36). And to the woman of Samaria, Jesus said: "Woman, believe me, the hour cometh, when ye shall neither in this mountain, nor yet at Jerusalem, worship the Father" (John 4:21).

The Gospels show Jesus receiving an offer of land and power, and refusing it: "And the devil, taking him up into an high mountain, shewed unto him all the kingdoms of the world in a moment of time. And the devil said unto him, All this power will I give thee, and the glory of them: for that is delivered unto me; and to whomsoever I will I give it. If thou therefore wilt worship me, all shall be thine. And Jesus answered and said unto him, Get thee behind me, Satan: for it is written, Thou shalt worship the Lord thy God, and him only shalt thou serve" (Luke 4:5–8).

There is surely no starker contrast in any other matter between the Old and New Testaments than there is in this matter of land, and power over land. In the Old Testament it is God who offers land to Abraham, and Abraham accepts; in the New Testament it is Satan who offers land to Jesus, and Jesus refuses. Furthermore, it seems from the story, as it appears in the Gospel according to Luke, that it is Satan, not God, who claims such matters at his disposition: "for that is delivered unto me," says Satan.

It is *almost* as if Jesus were saying that the Being who made the promises of land to Abraham, Isaac, Jacob, and the Israelites was the Devil, not God. But Jesus does not in fact say so, and his rejection of the satanic temptation is couched in terms of the Law of Moses. The Old Testament, interpreted in a Christian sense, remains of divine inspiration. But the combination of religion with nationalism, which appears so clearly in the Old Testament, disappears in the New. The early Christians allegorized and spiritualized the Old Testament right out of this world and into the next. The Promised Land, which the Patriarchs took to be Canaan, turns out to be Heaven. The early Christians, as well as spiritualizing the Old Testament, also internationalize it. The *real* Chosen People are no longer the Jews but all those—of whatever language, culture, or nation—who know themselves to be redeemed by Christ's sacrifice on the Cross. That is the new Covenant, which the older covenants are there to prefigure.

There is some internationalism—or what looks like internationalism—as well as an awful lot of nationalism in the Old Testament, and Saint Paul latched on to whatever internationalism he could find there. Thus, in his Epistle to the Galatians, Paul quotes from God's words to Abraham, as reported in Genesis (15:6): "Even as Abraham believed God, and it was accounted to him for righteousness. Know ye therefore that they which are of faith, the same are the children of Abraham. And the scripture, foreseeing that God would justify the heathen through faith, preached before the Gospel unto Abraham *saying,* In thee shall all nations be blessed. So then they which be of faith are blessed with faithful Abraham" (Gal. 3:6–9).

But of course Paul does not quote any of those passages in which God promises land to a particular people, or in which God conditionally exalts that people above others. As, for example, Exodus 19:5–6: "Now therefore, if ye will obey my voice indeed, and keep my covenant, then ye shall be a peculiar treasure unto me above all people: for all the earth *is* mine. And ye shall be unto me a kingdom of priests, and an holy nation." Nor does he take account of the many passages in which the Israelites are promised or given victory over their Gentile enemies.

The God of the Old Testament limits the covenant promise to the circumcised among the seed of Abraham (Gen. 17:10–14), but the New Testament abolishes that restriction.

In general it seems to me that those passages in the Old Testament that admit of a universalist or internationalist interpretation tend to be remote, vague, and contingent, whereas the nationalist passages are immediate, vivid, primary, and practical. It even seems to me that the internationalist passages may be little more than aspects of the nationalism, giving a universal extension to the mission of God's Chosen People. Later nationalisms were often universal, too, in that sort of way. You can find something of that spirit in the transactions of the founders of New England, in particular of the Bay Colony. When the great emigration from England to Massachusetts was under way in 1630, John Cotton, vicar of St. Botolph's Church at Boston in Lincolnshire, preached a famous farewell sermon to the Lincolnshire contingent of the emigrants from Southampton. He preached on the text, 2 Sam. 7:10: "Moreover I will appoint a place for my people Israel, and will plant them, that they may dwell in a place of their own, and move no more; neither shall the children of wickedness afflict them any more, as beforetime."

The Christian clergyman, like others of his persuasion in the seventeenth century, is claiming a Promised Land on the basis of an Old Testament text, construed terrestrially, and no longer figuratively. I shall soon consider some of the changes which had occurred in Christian society, and in Christianity, in the more than a millennium and a half that separate the Apostle Paul from the preacher at Southampton. But the point I am concerned with at the moment is that Cotton also introduces an internationalist note into his farewell sermon. He is concerned not only for the emigrants, but for the Indians whom the emigrants are about to displace. "Offend not the poor Natives," he said, "but as you partake in their land, so make them partakers of your precious faith."

Cotton of course was steeped in the Old Testament, and I think his advice concerning the Natives may be a fair sample of the references to blessings in store for the Gentiles which can be found in the Old Testament.

I must emphasize at this point what I am *not* trying to do in this chapter, for I may be in some danger of misleading you. I am not setting out to engage in or lay the groundwork for some kind of polemic against or mockery of the ancient Jews, or the early Christians, or the Puritans, or anyone else. Nor am I concerned with attacking either religion or even nationalism. I am trying to analyze certain relations between religion and nationalism. In the course of this attempt, certain anomalies and ironies appear. I find such anomalies and ironies illuminating in relation to my subject matter, and I cite them for that reason, and certainly not in order to score adversarial points.

It seems to me that the strength of nationalism in the Old Testament is a major and basic fact of my subject. It seems to me also that it is a fact that has been to some extent obscured not merely by the spiritualist and internationalist bowdlerizing interpretations of the early Christians but by later developments as well. For a time indeed, in the sixteenth and seventeenth centuries, the Old Testament was read again in the sense of its apparent, literal meanings, including its national-ist meaning. Then the pendulum swung back. Enthusiasm went out of fashion, and the Old Testament along with it, in the aftermath of the religious wars. The philosophes laughed at the Old Testament—which was a lot safer, in eighteenth-century France, than laughing at the New. For the deist philo-sophes, the mainstream of the movement, the Old Testament God was a grotesque travesty of God, as He actually was. The true God, the God compatible with scientific discoveries, was a first Cause only, inconceivably remote, unspeakably dignified, and debarred from any form of intervention in earthly affairs, from the moment of Creation onward. Al-though they disliked Christianity, the philosophes were actu-ally extending the Christian tendency to spiritualization by spiritualizing God himself very nearly out of existence.

For the philosophes—especially Voltaire who was a notable snob—the God of the Old Testament is the vulgar God of a primitive tribe, in a remote and backward province of a great and civilized Empire. A God who goes clumping around Palestine, accosting elderly Jews and offering them parcels of real estate—what nonsense the whole thing is! thought the philosophes.

For Jews, who participated in the Enlightenment and benefited from some of its consequences, the attack of the philosophes struck home. In some early and some modern apologias for the Old Testament, the Chosen-People – Prom-ised-Land part is played down as representing an early phase in the evolution of a profoundly spiritual religion. This was a second wave in the spiritualization of the Old Testament.

And yet as a great modern authority on Judaism has said "Judaism is an earthy religion." The earthiness is part of its power, and the promise of the Land is part of the earthiness.

The early Christians tried to get rid of the earthiness, be-lieving that the earth itself was, in any case, about to end. But the earth stayed where it was, more or less, and many of the Christians came back to earth.

Before I sketch the developing interaction within Christendom between religion and territorial politics, out of which new nationalisms developed, I should like to make two general points: one about the scope and one about the character of this inquiry. As regards the scope, I am confining myself to the Judeo-Christian tradition, and to some interactions and mutations of religion and nationalism within that tradition. (I offer here and there a few illustrations from the world outside that tradition, but that is all.) But why restrict the inquiry? Have not religion and nationalism been at work throughout the world and in cultures that were not affected by emanations of the Judeo-Christian tradition until quite modern times, and then perhaps only superficially? Should we not take these cultures into account? I'm sure we should, or *someone* should, but I know I'm not able to. Even to explore these matters within the framework of *one* great culture is daunting enough. Perhaps scholars belonging to other cultures have undertaken, or will undertake, parallel inquiries.

Still, even though my ignorance limits the scope of this inquiry to the particular tradition to which most of us belong, the Judeo-Christian tradition, it may be that this is the tradition within which this particular interaction is most relevant. It is certainly the tradition from which these twin forces have manifested themselves with the greatest terrestrial impact and extension.

Islam, although officially hostile to Judaism and Christianity, which it claims to supersede, appears, culturally speaking, to be a product of the impact of the Judeo-Christian religious writings on the mind of Muhammad. And in whatever ways nationalism and universalism may have manifested themselves of old in the cultures of Asia and Africa, it is certain that the modern manifestations of those forces in those cultures are to a great extent shaped by the concepts and language in which those same forces found expression within the Judeo-Christian tradition. Both forms of internationalism—Marxism-Leninism—that officially dominate so large a part of the modern Far

East *and* the unavowed nationalism that has disrupted the Marxist-Leninist polities along territorial lines are largely products of the Judeo-Christian culture.

My second general point is about the character of this inquiry. I want to stress the peculiar slipperiness—the Protean character, if you will—of the concepts involved. Things slide and merge into other things, which would appear to be quite different, and even opposed; this is a field in which the dialectic gets particularly frisky. Category limits that may appear quite distinct and stable conceptually—as between religion, politics, land tenure, Enlightenment, ethnicity, and so on—become blurred and permeable as they manifest themselves in history. We have just seen how the earthiness of the Old Testament was exploded by the New, with the Promised Land, together with its capital, vanishing vertically into invisible Heaven, the New Jerusalem. We shall soon see the Promised Land coming down to earth again, eventually to this particular part of earth, where we are now.

But before I go on with my main line of inquiry, let me offer three examples of the instability and mutability of the concepts in question. The first two concern the grounds for ill-treatment, in Christian lands, of two sets of stigmatized peoples: Jews and blacks. In both cases the ill-treatment was originally justified on religious grounds. Jews deserved to be humiliated or tortured or burned because of their persistence in blaspheming against the divinity of Christ. Blacks deserved to be enslaved because they were heathens from Africa.

Then some Jews, and a great many blacks, accepted baptism and became Christians. According to the Christian religion, as taught by Saint Paul, these new Christians ought immediately to have been accepted into the Christian community of love and fellowship. But of course they weren't. New grounds for oppressing them were found.

The Spanish Inquisition discovered the principle of *Limpieza de Sangre,* purity of blood. The blood of a converted Jew was impure; even if he personally was not a blasphemer, his ancestors had been. So he could, indeed had to be, excluded from the Christian community. By the exact same reasoning, American slaveowners justified holding black Christians as slaves. They might be Christians *now*, but their ancestors had been heathens, and rightfully enslaved, and therefore so should they be.

Thus, out of the coupling of religion with ascriptive genetics, racism is born.

In a later, more secular age, the religious reason or pretext is discarded altogether, and the genetic element is found to be sufficient in itself. As Georg von Schoenerer, a leading Austrian and German anti-Semite of the late nineteenth century, put it: "What the Jew believes is neither here nor there—in the race lies the swinery." Hitler takes over from there.

Those two examples of the mutability of religious and ethnic criteria are clearly sinister. My third example concerns the mutability of religious and *political* orientations, and it is not sinister. In fact, personally, I find it rather amusing—and also moving. It concerns religion and politics in the writings of Mahatma Gandhi. Recently a student of religion, Jim Wilson, went through the eighty-seven volumes of Gandhi's collected works to find out what these writings might tell him about Gandhi's God. He was startled by what he found, and he reported his findings in a recent issue of the specialist periodical *Religion* under the startling title: "Gandhi's God—a Substitute for the British Empire?"

It seems that up to 1907 the young Gandhi had been a devout believer in the British Empire. During this period, Wilson found that the references to God in Gandhi's writings are rather few, and these tepid and conventional. But in 1907 the British Empire, being at the time bent on appeasement of the Afrikaners, let Gandhi down with a bump. And from that moment on, God took on an overwhelming importance in Gandhi's writings: the references to Him become frequent, passionate, anguished.

I am most grateful to Mr. Wilson for this discovery. But I

think the hypothesis of his title does not do full justice to the significance of his discovery. For surely what is going on in Gandhi's mind, as he turns away from the British Empire and appeals to God, has to be more dynamic and momentous than the mere acquisition of a "substitute," a sort of teddy bear. I have not read those eighty-seven volumes; but, like everyone else, I have some acquaintance with Gandhi's subsequent emergence as a great national leader. Wherever a leader of men has a God, that God is invariably encouraging him— impelling him along a chosen path and giving him strength to persevere along that path. And we know where Gandhi's path led him, terrestrially speaking.

So I suggest an alternative hypothesis, which I prefer to Jim Wilson's. It is a hypothesis that combines the Old Testament and the New, a Mosaic with a Pauline element. It is that Gandhi's God is leading the way, a pillar of cloud by day and a pillar of fire by night, toward the Promised Land of an Independent India, and toward the destruction of the British Empire, which Gandhi once adored.

Of course Gandhi would not have put it like that. He was a Hindu and—what is more to the point politically speaking— a leader of Hindus. But he was also an eclectic, and he knew his Bible. In any case, we know the fact of what he accomplished politically, and the fact that he believed he was doing God's will in that political work. I believe that in this case a kind of religious conversion was a catalyst in the mutation of a kind of universalism—faith in the British Empire—into Indian nationalism.

□

The decisive event in the territorialization, and ultimately the nationalization, of Christianity was the reception, beginning with Constantine and codified by Theodosius, of Nicene Christianity as the official cult of the Roman Empire. Christ had said that His kingdom was not of this world, but the cult of Christ now becomes that of a worldly empire and is about to become the cult of many kings and princes. And official Christianity has to adapt itself to the heritage of classical antiquity. Between the Christian and his God there is now inserted a political layer, first in the form of the Imperial Court. Eusebius of Caesarea wrote: "Invested as he is with a semblance [*mimesis*] of heavenly sovereignty, [the Emperor] directs his gaze above, and frames his earthly government according to the patterns of that divine original, feeling strength in conformity to the monarchy of God."

The new intermediate political layer between Earth and Heaven is continuous with the old pre-Christian Roman Empire, which, in its most admired aspects, becomes partly Christianized in retrospect. Addressing an ecclesiastical assembly, according to Eusebius, Constantine developed an exegesis of Virgil's Fourth Eclogue (line 5): *Magnus ab Integro saeclorum nascitur ordo.* The newborn "order of the ages" prophesied in the Fourth Eclogue is now identified with Christianity. This provided Christianity with classical legitimation, and made the Christian Emperor the fulfillment of the classical past, rather than a deviation from it. At the same time Christianity itself became contaminated—as some earlier Christians might have seen the nature of the change—by the classical and pagan heritage. And that heritage included the deliberately exalted Roman nationalism of the Age of Augustus.

The acceptance of Virgil as a central figure in the culture of medieval Christianity is of critical importance. In medieval iconography Virgil figures as a prophet, side by side with David and Isaiah. Not only the Fourth Eclogue but the Aeneid acquires quasi-Scriptural status. And the Aeneid is a school of Roman patriotism.

Virgil's special status long outlasted the Empire of Constantine and his successors; it even outlasted the Middle Ages. Italians like Dante were especially susceptible to nationalism in its Virgilian form. But other nations, too, could come to see themselves as the true heirs of the Empire, the new Romans. Medieval Germans saw themselves in that light; so did the French of the Revolutionary period; so did the Victorian English. And the American Founding Fathers, as we shall see, could think of Americans as being the true Chosen People, the new Israel, and also as transfigured Romans, the true objects of the Sibylline prophecy of the Fourth Eclogue.

Nothing in the classical heritage was equivalent to the Old Testament concept of the Covenant. Yet classical antiquity had its own way of linking the idea of a given land to the idea of the divine. This was the cult of heroes who had died for the *polis,* the *respublica,* or the *patria.* Pericles placed the first victims of the Peloponnesian War among the immortals. And Virgil's Aeneas saw on the Elysian Plains the spirits of those who had suffered for the fatherland, "their brows bound with snowy fillets," equivalents of martyrs' crowns. (The Aeneid has its own version of a Promised Land: Italy, as promised to the Trojans by the Cumaean Sybil.)

The classical cult of the patria and its martyrs was about to become part of the heritage of medieval Christianity, further despiritualizing it, localizing it, and binding it to the earth.

Initially, Christian thinkers had tried to cope with the cult of the patria by using the exact same strategy on what we may call the classical front as they had used on the Old Testament front. They had rejected the cult of the patria in its literal and earthbound sense, while adopting it in a new spiritual sense. Saint Augustine is explicit both about the rejection and about the adoption. "Why should that man be praised?" he asks, "Because he was a lover of his city? That he could be carnally . . . But he was not a lover of the city above." In Book V of the *City of God* Augustine cites the great deeds of individual Romans for their purely terrestrial patria in order to encourage Christians to even more heroic deeds for their *patria aeterna.*

So the Roman patria joins the Jewish Promised Land, and fuses with it in the Sky. Intellectually, and as an aspect of Christianity, the Augustinian celestial synthesis proved remarkably durable. Nearly a thousand years later Peter Abelard, in one verse of his great hymn *Sabbato ad Vesperas,* exhorts his hearers to lift up their minds to their patria in heaven and to return to the heavenly Jerusalem out of Babylonian exile.

Nostrum est interim mentem erigere
Et totis patriam votis appetere
Et ad Jerusalem a Babylonia
Post longa regredi tandem exsilia.

(We must lift up our mind / And seek the patria with all our vows / And return after long exile / Out of Babylon to Jerusalem.) The hymn is set to the beat of the march of those same legions who had destroyed the earthly Jerusalem more than a thousand years before.

Durable though the idea of the *patria aeterna* was, intellectually speaking, it was the *patria terrestris* that was gaining ground, appropriately enough, in practical ways throughout Christendom, and to some extent, intellectually.

The politicization of Christianity following the conversion of Constantine had produced the new, essentially territorial, notion of Christendom. Christendom inherited from Imperial Rome—in many ways, but most notably through Virgil—the notion of the transcendent importance of the terrestrial patria. But the letter of the New Testament was still there, as was the teaching of the Fathers, including Augustine, working against the terrestrial patria and attachment to carnal cities. The balance seems to have been tilted in favor of the terrestrial patria by a new force moving out of Arabia in a formidable assault on Christendom.

The great forcing-factor in what concerned the reemergence of the terrestrial patria within Christendom was the impact of Islam, with the response of the Crusades. It was not just the loss of the Holy Land, though that was of the highest importance. It was the loss of huge tracts of what had formerly been Christendom, on the east and the south, and the sense of the rest of Christendom as menaced. All that brought the attention of Christians, both lay and clerical, away from the sky and the *patria aeterna* and down to the earth, with the problems of how to hold on to land and how to get it back. Christendom— terrestrial Christendom—began to appear as patria. And within that larger patria there were other patriae struggling to get out.

The term patria is an elastic one, and its use in classical antiquity or in medieval times should not be identified with the *patrie* the French started singing about in April 1792. There is a discontinuity in extent, in stability of concept, and in degree of organization. The ancient patria could be a locality, or it could be coterminous with the res publica, the Roman Republic or Empire. In medieval times patria could be a city, or a province, or a village; only in the later Middle Ages is it beginning to be applied to a kingdom. But where the word patria is used with emotional connotations—as when people are prepared, or exhorted, to die for their patria—then it does not seem to matter whether the focus of such feelings is a city or a kingdom or a nation-state. In that sense there is a direct line from ancient through medieval to modern times; from the patria of Cicero and Horace—and before that, from the polis of Pericles—to the patrie of Rouget de Lisle.

As early as the ninth century A.D., we find a pope using the word patria, both in its Augustinian, or heavenly, sense and in a terrestrial sense, and using the heavenly sense to support the terrestrial one. Pope Nicholas I (858–867) promised the eternal patria, the celestial realms, to anyone who died "for the salvation of the patria" (*pro Salutatione Patriae*). The Pope did not explicitly define this second patria as earthly, but it clearly is; the eternal patria, being saved already, didn't need people to die for its salvation. The new patria is Christendom, land inhabited or formerly inhabited by Christians.

In a general sense the Crusaders were fighting for Christendom. In a more down-to-earth sense a Crusader was fighting for his feudal lord. The emphasis begins to shift away from Christendom-in-general to particular lords and lordships. At a council at Limoges in 1031 a vassal of the Duke of Gascony is instructed: "For your lord you will have to accept death . . . and for this loyalty you will become a martyr of God." Things continued in that direction until, as Ernst Kantorowicz puts it: "By the middle of the thirteenth century . . . the crusader idea of a holy war was all but completely secularized, and its place was taken by a quasi-holy war for the defence of the realm or of the nation."

It is in Italy and France that these forms of holy nationalism achieve their most emphatic expressions. An Italian, or pan-Italian, nationalism does not explicitly emerge until the Renaissance, with Machiavelli, but city-state holy nationalism achieves an almost manic intensity in the writings of the thirteenth-century Florentine thinker Remigio de Girolami, believed to have been Dante's teacher. Remigio taught that the patria, the city-state, comes second only to God, "for the similitude it has to God," and takes precedence over the individual and over the family. Earlier generations had believed, from Genesis on, that man, the individual human being, was made in God's image; now it was found that God's image is even more faithfully reflected in the mystical body of the patria than in man. In line with the logic of that, Remigio held that a citizen, in order to save his country, should even be prepared to accept his own personal damnation. (Remigio here anticipates by a couple of centuries Machiavelli's preference, in the dedication of *The Prince,* for *la patria* over "my own soul.")

Remigio may have been Dante's teacher, but Dante did not follow him to this extreme. Dante clearly shows that he regards the mere holding of such a view as meriting damnation. He puts "il Cardinale" (Ottaviano Degli Ubaldini) in the Sixth Circle of Hell, among the heretics. The Cardinal is famous for having said: "If I have a soul, I have lost it a thousand times over for the Ghibellines."

Yet Dante's damnation of the Cardinal surely should be understood as the rejection of an extreme, not of the tendency that was carried to that extreme. Dante puts in hell several people whom he admires and even loves; these figure mostly in the Sixth Circle, among the heretics, and in the Seventh Circle, among the violent. The outstanding example is Brunetto Latini, condemned to the Third Ring of the Seventh Circle, and hero of the magnificent Fifteenth Canto of the *Inferno*. This is the Canto which ends with the words:

> Poi si rivolse, e parve di coloro
> che corrono a Verona il drappo verde
> per la campagna; e parve di costoro
> quegli che vince e non colui che perde.

(Then he turned back, and seemed like one of those who run for the green cloth at Verona through the open field; and of them seemed he who gains, not he who loses.) Who would not choose to be damned—in a purely literary way of course—if he could earn an immortal epitaph which depicted him as looking like that while being baked forever in Hell?

Dante was a nationalist, but one who synthesized his nationalism with his religion, instead of setting one against the other. He was not, like Remigio, a Florentine nationalist, but a Roman one, imperial Italian. He was a Roman Catholic in a very special sense: the "Roman" standing for the political, the "Catholic" for the spiritual aspect of his faith. The *Commedia*, like the Aeneid, is an epic of holy nationalism. Virgil is Dante's guide, in more senses than one: his guide to Hell and Purgatory, and also his mentor in the Imperial Roman faith. At the end of the Inferno, in the pit at the bottom of the Ninth Circle, we have the vision of Satan, chewing eternally on the three arch-traitors: Judas, Brutus, and Cassius.

The sin against Julius is very nearly as heavy as the sin against Jesus; the balance between the political and the spiritual is very nearly even.

Similarly, in the Paradiso, the Canto of the Redemption (vii) is immediately preceded by the Canto of Justinian. Justinian is glorified as the Christian emperor who moved the Empire back to Rome from Constantinople, whither Constantine had removed it, "contrary to the course of Heaven" (para. vi, line 2). Canto vi is a monologue in which Justinian narrates the triumphs of "the sacred standard" of Rome, triumphs which now appear as part of the prehistory of Christianity. And in Canto xxvii, Saint Peter speaks of "the high providence which with Scipio defended at Rome the glory of the world."

It could be argued that Dante's vision, being imperial and universal, is quite distinct from nationalism. But this distinction cannot be sustained for long. Rather, Dante's imperialism and apparent universalism supplied the somewhat incongruous vehicle for his intense Italian/Roman nationalism. An Italian scholar has put this very well. Referring to Dante's ostensible cosmopolitanism, Domenico Comparetti writes:

> The feeling therefore which led Dante to his political Utopia was based, strangely enough, on that idea which rendered its realisation impossible—the idea of national individuality. However much he may say that he is a citizen of the world, his patriotic utterances, the predilection he shows in all his writings for the Latins, whether ancient or modern, his enthusiasm for that great Rome which is the glory of Italy, the intense ardour with which by precept and example he affirms the nobility of the Italian language, the terrible words in which he denounced those "abominable" ones who prefer other languages to their own, and many other like things, mark him out clearly as the greatest and the earliest representative of Italian national feeling, and show that he felt himself to be far more an Italian than a cosmopolitan.

Comparetti, as a late-nineteenth-century Italian, might be suspected of projecting the values of the Risorgimento back into the early fourteenth century. Yet a modern French scholar, Jacques Goudet, who has made a special study of Dante's politics, reaches essentially the same conclusion. Dante (according to Goudet), when he had come to know the powerful of the world, had to realize that the Holy Empire "is not universal and cannot be. Quite smoothly, and in the measure to which it identified itself with real history, the Empire of the *Divine Comedy* perhaps lost the characteristics of dream, and prepared itself for the condition of nation or *patria,* becoming, in an intelligent fidelity to the past, intuition or pre-intuition of future realities."

□

Holy nationalism never reached such intellectual heights in medieval France as in medieval Italy, but the French form of holy nationalism was much more formidable politically, because it became the ideology of a powerful territorial state. As this nationalism took theological rather than secular forms, it is not identical with modern nationalist ideology. But my argument is that the difference may not be so great as the contrasting categories "theological" and "secular" suggest.

The concepts of the holiness of the kingdom of France, and of the holiness of any war fought by France against anyone, Christian as well as infidel, are well established by the late thirteenth century. And whereas in the earlier part of the Middle Ages, holy nationalism had justified itself first by spiritualizing, then by localizing, the classical concept of the patria, by the late Middle Ages, Old Testament nationalism is beginning to be invoked as well. When, at the end of the thirteenth century, Philip IV of France went to war with the Flemings, a French cleric preached on 1 Maccabees 3:20–22: "*They* march against us in the plenty of pride and lawlessness . . . *We,* however, will fight for our souls and laws; and the Lord himself will crush them before our faces." This treatment of an Old Testament text in a literal, nonallegorical, and territorial-nationalist way may be seen as an index of how far medieval Christianity had gone, by the late thirteenth century, away from spiritualization and back toward earthiness.

Philip IV's preacher went on: "There is no doubt but that those who die for the justice of the king and realm of France shall be crowned by God as martyrs. He who carries war against the king [of France] works against the whole Church, against the Catholic doctrine, against holiness and justice, and against the Holy Land."

Of course if France was the Holy Land, its rivals had to be

unholy lands—and so they turned out to be. The French disliked the Holy Roman Empire, that being a German sort of thing, and Guillaume de Sauqueville, a French Dominican preacher of the same period, cried out: The Empire is evil!

(Perhaps someone should write a thesis about the influence of Guillaume de Sauqueville on Ronald Reagan.)

The position as regards the status of my subject in late medieval France has been summed up by the eminent American medievalist Joseph Reese Strayer as follows: "It was the union of the sacred king and the holy country which speeded the emergence of the French state at the end of the thirteenth century. In France, the religion of nationalism grew easily out of the religion of monarchy."

How many people believed all that? There is solid evidence that a great many people believed something like it in France by the fifteenth century. The evidence is in the declared faith of Joan of Arc, and in the responses of her contemporaries to that declared faith.

Joan, in her brief life, never learned to read or write. She told her accuser-judges in Rouen that she had learned her religion from her mother. So, humanly speaking, the fusion of religion and nationalism, which became literally incandescent in Joan, must have been well established in the French peasantry of this period. This is confirmed by the response of the ordinary people to Joan's account of her divine mission to save the kingdom of France. That the people's response to Joan's claims was overwhelmingly favorable is attested not only by her friends but by her enemies. After her death the Court of England addressed a manifesto in the name of the infant sovereign, Henry VI by the Grace of God King of England and France, to the Emperor and to the Kings and Princes of Christendom. In the course of this manifesto, designed to justify the burning of Joan, her overwhelming popularity for a time is admitted: "During one whole year, more or less, this woman seduced the people, coming very close to them, so much that most people straying from truth through rumours believed in the fabulous tales."

Joan's version of religious nationalism is similar to, but

subtly and significantly different from, that of the preachers of Philip IV more than a century earlier. They had stressed the king, mentioning the realm only in second place. With Joan the emphasis is invariably on the Holy *Kingdom* of France; the king seems to be seen as a necessary adjunct to the kingdom, a lieutenant—Joan uses the word once—through whose coronation (*sacre*) Jesus manifests his concern for the Holy Kingdom. When Joan speaks of her "Lord," the reference is always to Jesus Christ, never to her terrestrial lord, the king. At Vaucouleurs, Joan tells the Dauphin's servant, Baudricourt: "The kingdom didn't belong to the Dauphin but to his Lord; yet his Lord wanted the Dauphin to become King, and to have the Kingdom in trust."

From the very beginning, when the Archangel Michael appeared to her at Domremy, when Joan was about twelve years old, the concern was for the kingdom. Saint Michael told her about "the pity there was for the kingdom of France." Later, at the very pinnacle of her mission, on the day of the coronation of Charles VII in her presence at Reims, Joan dictated a letter which contains the fullest statement she has left of the governing concept behind her mission. The letter was addressed to the Duke of Burgundy, that mighty and rebellious vassal of the King of France. In it Joan tells the duke: "all those who make war in [on?] the Kingdom of France make war against King Jesus, King of Heaven and all the world, my rightful and sovereign Lord."

Joan's mortal enemies had their own form of religious nationalism. This generally did not become overt at her trial, which was conducted in ecclesiastical, and therefore universalist, terms, and mainly by French theologians allied or subservient to the English power. (*Au milieu des docteurs, des savants et des traîtres,* Péguy put it centuries later.) But there is just one point where the nationalism of Joan's real accusers, and real judges, breaks through the pseudotheological cover. Item XLIII of her indictment reads as follows: "Item, the said Jeanne has said and published that the saints, angels and archangels speak French and not English, affirming in this way that these holy beings do, to their shame, hold in hatred a Catholic Kingdom, given up to the veneration of all the saints, in accordance with the prescripts of the Church." No Frenchman, however pliable, could ever have thought of that one!

Joan's English enemies and their French agents agreed in regarding her as above all a seducer of the people, what would later be called a rabble-rouser. Although she is called by God to bring a king to be crowned, her popular appeal is potentially disruptive; her emphasis on the direct link between God and the kingdom—as distinct from the person of the king—is new and subtly subversive.

In the development of nationalism within a religious culture, Joan's form of nationalism may be seen as a move away from the "sacral kingship" stage, in the direction of a land-and-people cult, such as is celebrated in the *Marseillaise*. Certainly Joan is revered by later generations of French nationalists. The champion of the "holy kingdom" is beloved by Frenchmen who normally have little use for either holiness or kingdoms—or think they haven't. In the nineteenth century the determinedly secular, and generally anti-Catholic historian Jules Michelet, says: "Yes, according to Religion, according to *la Patrie,* Jeanne Darc was a saint."

For French Catholic nationalists, into our own time, the cult of Joan has helped to secure Catholicism as a national and exclusive religion, rather than a universal one. The great poetic celebrant of that cult was Charles Péguy, who wrote *Le Mystère de la charité de Jeanne D'Arc.* Péguy's Catholicism explicitly rejected the antinational position of early Christianity. "Happy are those," he wrote, "who died for carnal cities"— *heureux ceux qui sont morts pour des cites charnelles!*

The choice of the word "carnal" recalls Augustine the more firmly to reject his antinationalist teaching. Péguy taught that "the supernatural is itself carnal" and that God Himself does not know whether the love of one's country really must come after the love of God. The "tree of race" and the "tree of grace" are alike eternal.

□ 2

New Chosen Peoples, New Promised Lands

The Germans, on the eve of Martin Luther's Reformation, were the next people to discover their own peculiar holiness and destiny. Let me cite two examples. The first is a passage from Sebastian Brant's *The Ship of Fools* (1494), a very popular and influential work at the time. Brant is writing in praise of Emperor Maximilian, one of a succession of figures to whom the Germans looked during this period to restore the glory of the Holy Roman Empire and the German people.

> The Germans once were highly praised
> And so illustrious was their fame.
> The Reich was theirs and took their name;
> But soon we found a German nation
> That brought its own realm ruination . . .
> But all you lords, you states and kings,
> Do not permit such shameful things! . . .
> The noble Maximilian
> He merits well the Roman crown.
> They'll surely come into his hand,
> The Holy Earth, the Promised Land.

The author of *The Ship of Fools* was a cultivated man, a humanist. Another document shows the same sort of idea working at another level of society. In the work known as *The*

Book of a Hundred Chapters (around 1500) the anonymous writer known as "The Revolutionary of the Upper Rhine" held that "the German people had been the genuine Chosen People, not merely since Charlemagne but since the creation; that before the Tower of Babel, the language spoken by the human race had been German." (*Old High* German, presumably.)

That nationalism not only existed, but was highly excited, in pre-Reformation Germany can hardly be doubted. It seems a reasonable hypothesis that holy nationalism in Germany at the beginning of the sixteenth century may have helped prepare the way for the reception of Luther's defiance of the foreign authority of the Pope, and especially for Luther's translation of the Bible. "The word of God in the original German," as the Revolutionary of the Upper Rhine might have put it.

Yet even though German nationalism may well have helped to make Germany receptive of Luther's message, the message itself was not nationalistic. Luther's aim was to reform the *universal* Church, not to establish a separate national German Church. Some of his allies, including his earliest protector, Ulrich Von Hutten, were German nationalists, but Luther himself, as a spiritual leader, spoke in universal terms. Furthermore, the actual progress of the Reformation, soon challenged by the Counter-Reformation, brought shattering disaster to the hopes of German nationalism. By the end of the Thirty Years' War, Germany was split about evenly between north and south, along religious-political lines, as well as being fragmented into some two thousand territorial units.

In France also, the religious wars at one time appeared to threaten the existence of Europe's most powerful nation, home of Europe's most advanced nationalism. It must have seemed to many nationalistically minded people in continental Europe in the late sixteenth and early seventeenth centuries that religion and nationalism had become opposing forces.

And yet it was during this same period that the Reformed faith was providing the strongest stimulus to emerging nationalism in what were to become, successively, the two most powerful nations on earth· Britain and the United States.

If a country was so unlucky as to be evenly divided between partisans of the Reformation and of the Counter-Reformation, then of course the Reformation was a disaster, nationally speaking. But if a country knew which side it was on in the religious struggle, as, for example, both Spain and England did, then the post-Reformation situation was highly stimulating to nationalist feelings. The national enemy was also the religious enemy; God was manifestly on the side of His Holy Nation; the foreign devils were devils indeed. That much was true of nations on either side of the religious divide—of Spain, as well as of England. But there was an added specific element in the teaching of the Reformers which favored the growth of nationalism in Protestant lands, by providing nationalism with divine legitimation. This was the hostility of the Reformers to the excesses of medieval allegorization, and their new emphasis on the literal meaning of the Old Testament. The Reformers did not, as has sometimes been suggested, altogether reject typology. They agreed that, in certain cases, passages in the Old Testament were to be interpreted as "types" prefiguring an aspect of the Redemption. But they condemned the tendency to read the Old Testament consistently as allegory, and they redirected attention to the literal meaning of the text.

Typology in relation to the Old Testament originally seems to have been a product of the contact between Greeks and Jews in first-century Alexandria. Hellenized Jews had become ashamed of what they had come to regard as the barbaric aspects of their scriptures. These Jews had learned from the Greeks how to cope with their problem, for the Greeks had had a similar problem with passages in Homer, which seemed undignified to Greeks of a later age. They had dealt with the problem by the allegorical method, and the Alexandrian Jews now applied the same method to their scriptures. The early Christians, especially the Alexandrian Father Origen, then adopted it and Christianized the entire allegorical system.

Under the Alexandrian form of typology, widely prevalent during the Middle Ages, everything in the Old Testament prefigured something in the New. This had the effect of filtering nationalism out of the Bible. If everything in the Old Testament had to be taken as an allegorical prelude to the New, then nationalism was out, since it is either nonexistent or implicitly rejected in the New.

Medieval nationalism drew mainly on its Roman heritage, with the patria now arbitrarily associated with Jesus. Medieval writers of nationalist tendency knew and used the Old Testament, but drew their nationalist inspiration mainly from classical sources. The beasts at the opening of the *Inferno* are out of Jeremiah, but Dante's nationalism is nourished by Virgil.

Luther and Calvin, however, to the extent that they deallegorized the Bible, tended to reactivate the nationalism of the Old Testament. Calvin dismissed much allegory as "frivolous guesses." Luther said: "The literal sense of Scripture alone is the whole essence of faith." Hence the Old Testament was read literally, by people already predisposed to nationalism, and the Old Testament is full of nationalism and divine legitimation of nationalism.

Strangely enough, the chastening of the excesses of the old typology was followed in a relatively short time by the development of a new typology, no less exuberant than the old. The early Christians read the Old Testament as prefiguring the New. But the seventeenth-century Puritans, in old and New England, read the Old Testament as prefiguring themselves, and the lands of their sacrifices and labors.

Cromwell spoke of the English as "a people that have had a stamp upon them from God." He also said: "if any one whatsoever think the Interest of Christians and the Interest of the Nation inconsistent, I wish my soul may never enter into his or their secrets!" He told the Little Parliament: "Truly God hath called you to this work by, I think, as wonderful providences as ever passed upon the sons of men in so short a time . . . Truly you are called by God to rule with Him and for Him." And John Milton asked: "Why else was this nation chosen before any other, that out of her, as out of Zion, should be proclaimed and sounded forth the first tidings and trumpet of reformation of all Europe?" ("English nationalism never existed," according to Hugh Seton-Watson. You could have fooled me.)

The Counter-Reformation countries could not let the Protestants get away with being the new Israel, so on that side too the typological barrier began to come down. Or rather a new form of typology began to emerge, taking the Old Testament as prefiguring, no longer Christ, but whichever nation happens to be talking about itself. Moreover, continuity with Israel could be claimed by countries considering themselves oppressed as well as by countries in triumphant mood. In seventeenth-century Catholic Ireland, among a people suffering greatly from the effects of Cromwell's identification of the *English* with the Chosen People, a seventeenth-century Gaelic poet identified the *Irish Catholics* with those same versatile Israelites:

> Clann Israel uair san Eigipt.
> Fa an-bhruid nirt námhad De . . .

(The Children of Israel once in Egypt, / under the oppression of the strength of the enemies of God . . .) Cromwell thought of himself as an Israelite, but the Irish *knew* he was really an Egyptian.

But in the main, identification with Israel and the new nationalistic typology remained a Protestant property, and a constant theme of Protestant discourse. By about 1630 it appeared that God had chosen not one but two Protestant English-speaking peoples. The earliest settlers in New England had been brought up to think of themselves as part of a Chosen People in England, and some of them—though probably not most of them at this early stage—thought of themselves as going to a Promised Land. John Cotton, in the farewell sermon at Southampton in 1630 quoted in Chapter 1, preached from a Promised Land text. There is reason to suspect, however, that Cotton's words may not have struck quite the right note to the ears of those responsible for the expedition.

The leaders of the settlers, being prudent as well as brave, did not wish their followers to think that all was about to be made easy by the assurance of divine aid. On the contrary, they wanted their followers to know from the start that things were going to be hard.

In Governor Bradford's account of the landing of the Pilgrim Fathers, the notion of Plymouth as a Promised Land is explicitly rejected: "Besides what could they see but a hideous and desolate wilderness, full of wild beasts and wild men? . . . Neither could they, as it were, go up to the top of Pisgah to view from this wilderness a more Godly country to feed their hopes (Deut. 3:27), for which way soever they turned their eyes (save upward to the heavens) they could have little solace or content in respect of any outward objects." And Governor Winthrop, in *A Model of Christian Charity,* written aboard the *Arbella* bound for Massachusetts Bay, stresses the need for "strict performance" by the settlers of their side of the covenant with God, if they are to expect the grace, rather than the wrath of God. "We shall find that the God of Israel is on our side when ten of us shall be able to resist a thousand of our enemies." In its context, that sounds much more like a warning than a promise.

It was only as the wilderness began to be subdued that people began to become confident about identifying New England with the Promised Land. Richard Mather, a spiritual leader of the original settlers, lived long enough to sense the new mood and to be troubled by it. In a sermon of 1650, Richard Mather, as Robert Middlekauff, biographer of the Mathers, puts it, "reminded his church that men must not confuse holiness with geography." Holiness, did not reside in the landscape, "neither Jerusalem nor any other place" was holy.

But the thing was too strong. Richard Mather was not even able to save his own son, Increase, from confusing holiness with geography. In a 1677 sermon Increase Mather asked: "Where was there ever a place so like unto new Jerusalem as New England hath been?" Twenty years later, dismayed—as his father had been long before—by evidence of increasing worldliness, Increase Mather suggested that New England "served the Lord as a type of Hell, an emblem for the edification of other nations still capable of profiting by its dismal example."

The "dismal example" theory did not catch on; the Promised Land theory did. It is remarkable that, as the influence of religion in general weakened in the second half of the eighteenth century, confidence in the proposition of America as the Promised Land appears stronger than it was among the Puritan Fathers. It is almost as if the object of faith is shifting from Heaven to earth, in an emerging cult of America itself, with the notion of the Promised Land there as a bridge, joining the memories of the old religion to the reality of the new, and also as a veil, obscuring the transformation of the object of worship.

Faith in America the chosen was manifest on the eve of the Revolution, and during its course. In November 1775 Ebenezer Baldwin prophesied: "I would suppose these colonies to be the foundation of a great and mighty empire; the largest the world ever saw, to be founded on such principles of liberty and freedom, both civil and religious, as never before took place in the world; which shall be the principal seat of that glorious kingdom which Christ shall erect upon earth in the latter days." On 16 March 1776 the Continental Congress resolved "that it may please the Lord of Hosts, the God of America, to animate our officers and soldiers with invincible fortitude, earnestly beseeching him to . . . grant that a spirit of incorruptible patriotism and undefiled religion may universally prevail."

Patriotism and religion are fused in that momentous hour in the service of the Lord of Hosts, the God of America.

After the Revolution, Timothy Dwight, later President of

Yale, and an indefatigable versifier of verse, celebrated George Washington in the role of Joshua, conqueror of the new Canaan.

> The chief whose arm to Israel's chosen Band
> Gave the fair empire of the Promised Land
> Ordain'd by Heaven to hold the sacred sway
> Demands my voice and animates my lay.

"Animates" may be pitching it a bit high, but you get the idea.

While the Promised Land identification was taking hold, the concept of the Chosen People had shifted. In the beginning, both in England and in New England, the Chosen were a spiritual elite, "visible saints," those who had undergone, or were believed to have undergone, conversion to a living faith in Christ. But the acceptance of infant baptism by the second half of the seventeenth century made the "visible saints" concept impossible to sustain in practice, though it was defended in theory long after it had in fact broken down. In the late seventeenth century, Solomon Stoddard of Northampton was teaching that "the entire nation comprised the Church, because the entire nation, saints and sinners alike, enjoyed a special covenant with God." This was revolutionary doctrine in terms of earlier Puritan teaching, though some English Puritans, under Oliver Cromwell, seemed to have been moving in the same general direction. In New England, Increase Mather resisted the Stoddard doctrinal innovations. But Stoddard's doctrine of "saints and sinners alike" fell in with the logic of infant baptism, and the demands of parents to have their children baptized were so strong as to prevail over the misgivings of the clergy.

Babies were now members of the Chosen People. And babies are *not* saints, visibly or audibly.

□

We have already contemplated the phenomenon of the perceived genetic transmission of *un*holiness in the cases of Jews and blacks. In seventeenth-century New England we can contemplate the phenomenon of the perceived genetic transmission of *holiness*. (Not in strict theory of course, since baptism, not birth, brought the child within the covenant, but since baptism followed automatically on birth, the theoretical distinction lacked practical significance.)

"Christenings make not Christians." Roger Williams, the most determined American opponent of the tendency toward sanctified nationalism, said that. Williams is, I think, the most determined, eloquent, and consistent antinationalist to appear anywhere.

In our own time Simone Weil went to greater lengths in the sheer fervor of her antinationalism. But hers was a self-destructive fervor, a disgust for all forms of human bonding, which culminated in fasting to death. The antinationalism of Roger Williams, on the other hand, was compatible with life, and even with some very shrewd politicking and diplomacy.

Williams, being among those who like to read the Bible and make up their own minds, disregarded the deallegorizing of Luther and Calvin; wholeheartedly interpreted the Old Testament in the old typological way, as predictive of the New; and at the same time adamantly opposed the new nationalistic typology of contemporary Puritans like John Cotton. His strict typological approach, like that of some of the early Fathers, filtered nationalism out of the Old Testament. But even filtered, the Old Testament, according to Williams, was not really necessary: "Christ Jesus and his Testament are enough for Christians, although we had never heard of Moses" or "the whole Old Testament." Basing himself on the New Testament alone, Williams resisted the nationalizing tendencies in Britain and America. In 1644, in a letter to "the Commissioners of the General Assembly (so-called) of the Church of Scotland," he posed this question: "Where find you evidence of a whole nation converted to the Faith . . . ?" He wrote of "the great Mysterie of the Church's sleepe," when, after Constantine, "the Leaders of Christ's Churches turned into the Wildernesse of National Religion." "The *bodies* of all nations," said Williams, "are a part of the *world,* and although the Holy Spirit of God in every nation where the Word comes washeth white some Blackamores and changeth some Leopard spots, yet the bodies and bulks of nations cannot by all the Acts and Statutes under Heaven put off the Blackamore skin and the Leopard spots." Specifically addressing himself to New England, he wrote that Canaan ought not to be taken as "a Pattern for all Lands; it was a non-such," and when the Bay Colony used the pattern of Israel, "here they lost the path and themselves!" Nationalism appeared to Williams as one among a number of symptoms of a general idolatry, which a later age would call materialism. "The truth is," he wrote, "the great Gods of this world are God-belly, God-peace, God-wealth, God-honor, God-pleasure, etc." And, for New England, he added to the list: "God Land." I take him to have had in mind both idolatry of land in general and also that idea of a divine promise of land, the idea for which the Bay Colony had "lost the path and themselves."

Roger Williams' teachings on the separation of church and state are a familiar and respected landmark in the approved American cultural retrospect. His vigorous assaults on divinely sanctioned nationalism have left much less of a mark, though they formed the basis of his teachings on church and state. Apparently his utterances on "the Wildernesse of National Religion" remained inaudible, even to editors of his collected work. The seven-volume edition published in the 1960s and currently in use incorporates in facsimile the text of the six-volume nineteenth-century Narragansett edition.

The introduction to that collection quotes, without any qualifying note by either nineteenth-century or twentieth-century editor, a poem by John Durfee, which depicts the great seventeenth-century dissident as a stock Puritan out of Central Casting, a typological nationalist cherishing the conventional Israelite analogy.

> Beside the good man lay his Bible's fair
> Broad open page upon the accustom'd stand

> And many a message had he noted there
> Of Israel wandering the wild wastes of sand
> And each assurance had he marked with care
> Made by Jehovah of the promised land.

In the context it is made clear that the promised land is now New England. The conversion of Roger Williams into a Chosen-People – Promised-Land buff is a conspicuous miracle of holy nationalism. Williams' teaching on these matters had been neither accepted nor rebutted, but his person had been iconographically incorporated into the tradition which he abhorred, and which had prevailed.

□

The specific linkage with ancient Israel long endured, though it became less conspicuous outside New England, and in a developing and partially more secular America, containing a high proportion of non-Protestants. But the basic notion of the United States as a nation peculiarly blessed by God not only survived but flourished exceedingly. The new immigrants took to the notion of the holy nation like ducks to water. Or rather, in many cases new immigrants, like the Puritan settlers themselves, brought faith in a holy nation—Ireland or Poland, say—along with them, and simply transferred its location, along with their persons, without necessarily being aware that they were doing so.

Basically the immigrants made only one stipulation concerning the holy nation: that the holy nation had henceforward to be understood as including *them*. This stipulation was not always easily made good; and before it was, the immigrants had to make concessions, adapting themselves to an American ethos of Protestant formation. In the late nineteenth century John Ireland, Catholic Archbishop of St. Paul, Minnesota, liked to stress that America had been shaped by the Puritans. He was telling his flock something about what they had to adapt themselves to. And they did. Of the more successful cases of adaptation, one might almost say that an American

Catholic is a Protestant who goes to Mass. The name of John F. Kennedy comes to mind.

But it was more than just a matter of immigrants imitating Puritans retrospectively. The nineteenth-century immigrant experience in itself resembled that of the Puritans in some basic ways. In "Religion and Ethnicity in America," Timothy Smith argued that "the acts of uprooting, migration, resettlement, and community building became for the participants a theologizing experience." He also argues:

> From its colonial beginnings, the migration of bonded groups or the formation of such groups in the new land made the biblical imagery of the Exodus seem a metaphor for the American experience, not only for English Puritans and Russian Jews, but for Christian villagers of Catholic, Protestant, and Orthodox persuasions from all parts of Europe.
>
> Linking the American future with the Kingdom of God was not, therefore, an exclusively Yankee obsession, nor the Social Gospel a Protestant preserve. Jews of both Reform and Orthodox faith, radical Irish as well as Chicano Catholics, and Mormon converts from Europe . . . have also been people of the dream.

Nor was it enough to be also "people of the dream." The new dreamers had to convince the children of the old dreamers that they were all part of the same dream. That has been a slow process, and it is still continuing. Consider the curious history of the Irish Catholic breakthrough in our own time. In the mid-twentieth century, Francis, Cardinal Spellman, of New York, had the word "Americanism" constantly on his lips, as if it were some venerable dogma of the Catholic Church. The Cardinal's use of "Americanism" was, I think, significantly more subtle than he made it sound, which was *not* particularly subtle. In his explicit and ostensible use of the term, the enemy was Communism. "Americanism" was made up of two elements: patriotism and religious faith. Atheistic Communism was the double and deadly enemy of "Americanism" in all that the word stood for: hostile both to the United States itself and to all the religions represented there.

That was the message, or rather the surface of the message. Beneath the surface there were other messages, more directly relevant to American society, and especially to intergroup competition in American society. First, the identification of religious faith of some kind as an essential component in Americanism would be accepted by most Americans. But that identification tended to exclude and isolate one important group: the liberal and secular element in the establishment, of Protestant background but agnostic or vaguely deist in outlook. These people were necessarily deficient in Spellman's Americanism, since they rejected its religious component. Might they not be deficient also in relation to the other component: patriotism? What about Alger Hiss?

It was not the Cardinal's role to make such connections explicitly. That job was ably handled by Senator Joseph R. McCarthy. McCarthy deftly smeared that pillar of the liberal establishment, Adlai Stevenson, by means of "a slip of the tongue": "Alger, I mean Adlai."

Spellman and McCarthy were squeezing an old and uncomfortable boot onto a new foot. For generations the WASP establishment had treated Catholics—Irish Catholics especially—as somewhat less than 100 percent Americans; the faith of Catholics put their loyalty in question. Now the tables were turned. Catholics were emerging as 100 percent Americans, and they were casting doubt on the loyalty of members of the WASP establishment, whose *lack* of faith put their loyalty in doubt.

In this exercise, Joe McCarthy's sheer outrageousness was, in the early years of his notoriety, helpful to Catholics. He provoked the liberal establishment into replying, copiously, and often into attacking Catholics and Catholicism, as well as the extremism of the McCarthyite version of anti-Communism. But for Catholics to be denounced as extreme anti-Communists could only be helpful to them, in the political and emotional climate of the mid-twentieth century. Many Protestants also suspected the liberal elite of being soft on Communism. McCarthy became the first American Catholic politician to acquire a large and enthusiastic national following among American Protestants as well as Catholics. He was destroyed, in his suicidal attack on the best-defended institutional bastion in America: the Pentagon. But McCarthyism, as a social and political movement, has to be classified, I believe, as a success: a disreputable sort of success, to be sure, but so are many other sorts of successes. McCarthyism was an engine for the social promotion of Catholics in America and the promotion of Irish Catholics in particular. McCarthy, backed by Spellman, conveyed to millions of non-Catholic anti-Communist Americans the novel idea that Catholics were a specially reliable, and especially tough, breed of anti-Communist.

Some time around 1950 many Americans, with the aid of Joe McCarthy, discovered that the Antichrist had changed his address, moving from the Vatican to the Kremlin. This discovery significantly enhanced the social and political status of Catholics in America.

Personally, I believe that without Joe McCarthy's crusade in the 1950s, John F. Kennedy could not have been elected in 1960. The contrast in styles must have helped. Joe McCarthy was the tough cop, whose ugly goings-on prepared the way for the breakthrough of the nice (but equally anti-Communist) cop, Jack Kennedy. Kennedy's liberal admirers were pained by his refusal to attack McCarthy. But Kennedy may well have been less interested in being admired by liberals than he was in being elected President of the United States. And if he had attacked McCarthy, he would have destroyed his own political base in Massachusetts—where there were more McCarthyites than in any other state in the Union—and could not have been elected President.

In terms of my general theme, let me offer an image that

may contain an element of exaggeration, but which is, I think, suggestive as to the realities.

Before the McCarthy-Kennedy breakthrough of 1950–1960, American Catholics had their tents pitched in the courtyard of the temple of the holy nation. After that breakthrough, there is a Catholic altar in the temple itself. Catholics are now among the "visible saints" of the national religion. The founders of the Bay Colony must be wondering at what God hath wrought.

It might be thought that the use of the term "national religion" applied to a country which does not have a national church is inappropriate. Yet the term "national religion"—as well as being used by Roger Williams in a derogatory sense—was used in the United States more than a hundred years ago, in very much the same sense I am using it now. It appeared in an 1858 *Harper's* article, "Providence in American History." The author of the article held that the fundamentals of American democracy developed from the idea of a Kingdom of God on earth, and that this idea is still present in the "national religion," distinct from, and in fact opposed to, the idea of a national church. He writes: "A national Church is one thing, a national Religion quite another; and in nothing are they more unlike than in their capacity to awaken the sense of Providence in the breast of a people." Ernest Lee Tuveson, who quotes the article, does not regard this opinion as unrepresentative of American attitudes for the period. Rather, he thinks it epitomized "the dominant contemporary attitude." The author of "Providence in American History" saw the American Constitution, despite its secular language and tenor, as the sacred document of the national religion. "The American Constitution," he says, "has a moral meaning, a sacredness, over and above what political science and civil compacts can ever give to the organic law of a commonwealth." In that matter, too, the article, Tuveson believes, "undoubtedly expressed a widespread conviction."

This nineteenth-century author appears more securely confident than were several seventeenth-century Puritans in the belief that America is indeed the Promised Land and Holy Land, for he concludes: "And it is true of our land as of Horeb. 'Put off thy shoes from thy feet for the land whereon thou standest is holy ground' (Exod. 3:5)."

Yet this author is less jingoistic than a modern reader of that passage might infer, for he feels the need for a belief in Providence as a check on the hubris latent in American nationalism. "If," he writes, America "depended exclusively on [human instrument elites], or if it leaned upon them in such a way as to banish the thought of God . . . then it would idolize itself and its machinery."

The outbreak of the American Civil War, just three years after the publication of "Providence in American History," might seem to refute the writer's thesis about the power of the American national religion. Yet the course and outcome of the Civil War may, with better warrant, be seen as confirming the strength of the national religion. Paul D. Escott shows with what deep misgivings and soul-searching, not only Robert E. Lee, but Jefferson Davis also, approached the breach with the United States; how many large groups and regions wavered; how, despite the efforts of the pulpits of the South and some of the press, Confederate nationalism never prevailed over states' rights; and how, toward the end, soldiers of the Confederacy were voting with their feet for peace and reintegration into the United States.

It was the Civil War, too, that gave the national religion its anthem of victory: "The Battle Hymn of the Republic."

The national religion of the author of "Providence in American History" was definitely Protestant: more precisely pan-Protestant. Today, although still mainly Protestant, the national religion—civil religion, if you prefer—can probably be defined as pan-Christian, rather than pan-Protestant. The national religion is often evoked in Judeo-Christian terms, but I think that is big-city usage, more or less in the way that ecumenical concepts embracing Catholics as well as Protestants were exclusively big-city stuff in the first half of this century.

I hesitate to suggest that the Jews need a Joe McCarthy. But it is true that, in relation to such matters, God does indeed move in a mysterious way His wonders to perform.

□

It may be appropriate at this point for me to say something about what I feel personally, in relation to these, the wonders of holy nationalism. Up to now I have been attempting to analyze these phenomena mainly in historical terms. But value judgments cannot be kept out altogether, and it is better to make them explicit. So let me try to explain where I stand vis-à-vis holy nationalism—although the ground is exceedingly slippery to stand on.

In my own country I am regarded as distinctly weak on holy nationalism, in both its constituent departments. I am, I believe, the only professed agnostic ever to be elected to Dáil Eireann. (I don't say the only agnostic ever to be elected; that is quite a different matter. How many of those there may be, God only knows!) I have also offered over the last sixteen years a sustained critique of the Irish nationalist ideology, Irish Republicanism, whose most passionate adherents are the Provisional IRA.

Here the going gets particularly slippery. For in any formal sense Irish Republicanism is not a *holy* form of nationalism. It is secular in form, a product of the Enlightenment and of French Revolutionary ideas as diffused by Theobald Wolfe Tone and others. It originated among deists and agnostics drawn from the Irish Protestant community, and claims to transcend the old sectarian differences, substituting for them "the common name of Irishman," a secular national identity.

I could be reasonably happy with that ideology, if it was for real, which it has not been for a long time. The reality, beneath an increasingly perfunctory pseudosecular cover, is Irish Catholic holy nationalism. The real founder and exemplar of modern Irish Republicanism is not the skeptical Wolfe Tone but the mystical martyr Patrick Pearse, with his emotional fusion of Catholicism and nationalism, a fusion closely resembling that which obsessed and inspired his French contemporary, Charles Péguy.

I see Pearse's Republicanism today as fueling a long-drawn-out, cruel, and sordid religious war between Catholics and Protestants in Northern Ireland. Of course it is not a purely religious war; no religious war was ever pure. But religion defines the parties to the struggle, and holy nationalism supplies a large part of the motivation. Among some, though by no means all, of the combatants, there is a will to martyrdom that rivals that of members of the Hizbollah, the Party of Allah, in Lebanon. The late Bobby Sands was a case in point. He and his admirers saw him as reenacting in his hunger strike the passion and death of Jesus Christ, for the sacred cause of Ireland.

I dislike and fear the variety of manic holy nationalism which afflicts my own country. So I tend to contemplate with some degree of aversion, manifestations of holy nationalism in other people's countries also. I am reminded of a Spanish story I heard from my wife. A visiting English clergyman was trying to convert to Protestantism a young anarchist bootblack. The bootblack would have none of it. "How can I believe in *your* religion," he asked, "when I don't even believe in my own, which is the only one, and the true one?" (*Que es la única y la Verdadera.*) So how can I believe in *your* nationalism when I don't even believe in my own?

□

Yet there is a sense in which we all have to believe in nationalism, for, as Carlyle advised the American transcendentalist Margaret Fuller to continue accepting the universe: "Madam, you'd better."

It seems impossible to conceive of organized society without nationalism, and even without holy nationalism, since any nationalism that failed to inspire reverence could not be an effective bonding force. Suppose that a virus destructive of reverential nationalism were to become pandemic in the United States. In consequence, your flag becomes no more meaningful in your eyes than any other piece of colored cloth, your Constitution no more venerable than any other antique document. Would rationality, self-interest, and pragmatism continue to hold you together, or would you burst apart, once you had lost the common bond of national religion? My guess is that you would burst apart.

I find the religion of Roger Williams more impressive and attractive, intellectually and morally, than that of Solomon Stoddard and the other holy nationalists. But the United States is much more the creation of the holy nationalists than it is of Roger Williams.

It might be nice if loyalty to particular nations were superseded by loyalty to the human race. I say *might* because I do not know. Frightful things have been done in the name of loyalty to a particular nation, but then frightful things have also been done in the name of universalist doctrines: Catholicism, Communism. In any case, despite a fair amount of "one world" and "global village" rhetoric, there are no signs, at the United Nations or anywhere else, of any real movement in the direction of superseding nationalism.

"Respect, but suspect" was a favorite saying of David Ben-Gurion to his followers. He used it with reference specifically to the United States; but it seems good advice in approaching any nationalism. To use an old analogy: the stuff is like fire; you need it to warm you, but it can destroy you if it gets out of control.

In conclusion, I should like to distinguish between three kinds of holy nationalism. These can be ticketed, in ascending order of arrogance and destructiveness, "chosen people," "holy nation," and finally "deified nation," the most manic malign and literal version of God Land. The idea of "chosen people" contains within itself not only national pride, but also humility, anguish, fear, and guilt. The chosen people can rightly be punished, and God can use other peoples as instruments of their punishment. Or, as Thomas Hooker and others taught, God, having chosen one people, can simply drop it for another. Just as He dropped the Jews for the Christians, and the

English for the Americans, so He could even drop the Americans for some other nation. (For some reason, Hooker fancied the Turks.)

The idea of "holy nation"—that is, chosen people with tenure—is getting dangerously near to the third category. But the holy nation is still under God, even if basking in His permanent favor.

When the third category is reached there is no longer any entity, or law, or ethic superior to the nation. Therefore, whatever the nation decides to do, or whatever its leader does in the name of the nation, is inherently and intrinsically right, however it may appear to other peoples, who have by definition no rights, since all rights belong to the nation alone. This was the holy nationalism of the Third Reich: "The nation idolizing itself."

As usual, the categories are unstable, slippery. And within the two first categories of holy nationalism there is, I think, always at least a little deified nation, screaming to be let out.

□ 3

Puritanism, Enlightenment, Nationalism

The American Revolution and the French Revolution are, I believe, more symmetrical in their intellectual origins than is usually acknowledged. In the intellectual ferment preceding those two great revolutions, three major forces can be seen at work, in varying forms of combination and interaction: Puritanism, Enlightenment, and Nationalism.

The importance of Puritanism in the prehistory of the American Revolution has been long and amply acknowledged, by friend and foe alike, and most notably by certain of the Founding Fathers. The early settlers in New England were seceding from the British polity of that time on religious grounds, and the later political secession, preceded as it was by intense religious controversy and agitation, can be seen as a kind of continuation and consequence of that earlier secession. It was so seen by John Adams, who wrote to Thomas Jefferson in 1818: "I think with you that 'it is difficult to see at what point the Revolution began.' In my Opinion it began as early as the first Plantation of the Country." Tocqueville put it: "The whole destiny of America is contained in the first Puritan who landed on these shores."

□

The part played by Puritanism, in both its Protestant and Catholic forms, helped prepare the way for the French Revolu-

tion—or, to use Edmund Burke's subtly different and sometimes preferable formula, the Revolution in France. Puritanism's eighteenth-century role may be considered under two
heads: Puritanism-outside-the-Enlightenment and Puritan-
ism-within-the-Enlightenment. But whether working from
outside or inside the Enlightenment, Puritanism tended to
stimulate nationalism in late-eighteenth-century Europe, just
as it had done in seventeenth-century England and just as it
was doing in late-eighteenth-century America.

The carriers of unenlightened Puritanism who played a major role in the undermining of the ancien régime were the
Jansenists. These were Catholic Puritans, who remained
within the fold of the Catholic Church—although just barely,
and with notable and relevant reservations. Although the Jansenists remained Catholics, an American Puritan could recognize them as kindred spirits, and as a leaven within the Catholic world. In the MAGNALIA CHRISTI AMERICANA (1702),
Cotton Mather wrote: "the Papists in Europe have grown better of late years, by the growth of Jansenism among them." In
the late seventeenth and early eighteenth century, the aging
Louis XIV, under the influence of Jesuit confessors and of
Rome, had broken up the Jansenist religious houses and otherwise persecuted Jansenists. Eighteenth-century Jansenists had
reason, therefore, to resent the French monarchy, the Papacy,
and the Jesuits. How deep their resentment went and how
efficiently they could bring it to bear, they proved, in the
1760s, when they achieved the ruin of the Jesuit order and the
expulsion of the Jesuits from France. The Jansenists were able
to do this because of their strength in the legal profession and
their predominant influence over the legal institutions of
France, the parlements. The king could not lawfully collect
new taxes unless they were registered by the parlements. The
leverage which that gave to the parlements helped tilt the scale
in favor of the Jansenist influence. And when the Jesuits were
so imprudent as to take legal proceedings before a parlement,
they delivered themselves into the hands of their enemies.

All this was not simply a matter of paying off old scores, though that entered into it. There was also a large issue of principle involved. The Jansenists saw themselves as defending the liberties of the Gallican church against the unlawful encroachment of the papacy and of its international *corps d'elite,* the Jesuits. The French monarchy had connived at those encroachments, but now upright French Christians, interpreting with integrity the laws of France, recalled the reigning monarch to his duty.

All in all, it was a signal victory for French nationalism, against the universalist forces of the Counter-Reformation. It was, at the same time, a shaking of the foundations of Throne and Altar in France itself: humiliation of the monarchy; and reduction of the political, social, and intellectual influence of the Catholic Church. The expulsion of the Jesuits from France should be seen as a major politico-religious seismic wave, preceding the great earthquake that came a quarter of a century later, in 1789.

The philosophes, proud carriers of the Enlightenment, were divided in their opinions about the affray between Jesuits and Jansenists. Voltaire disliked Jansenists a lot more than he did Jesuits. Eighteenth-century Jesuits were somewhat worldly people, even anxious to be part of the Enlightenment in their own way. Jansenists, on the other hand, reeked of the previous century and its persecuting ardor. As for the parlements, they were the principal engines of religious persecution in eighteenth-century France. So Voltaire's personal views were mildly pro-Jesuit, though he did not enter into the public controversy. When the actual expulsions occurred he took a Jesuit into his own home, just across the border from France. He thus made a characteristically Voltairean point, full of tolerance and irony, at the expense of both sets of Christian disputants and of the ancien régime in general.

Other philosophes were more militant and less complicated. D'Alembert publicly rejoiced, in a pamphlet. The Jansenists didn't matter, he thought; they were figures out of the past.

The Jesuits, on the other hand, were insidious enemies. Had they not tried to take over the Encyclopédie itself, and the entire Enlightenment along with it? In any case, the expulsion had been a blow to the Roman Catholic Church, therefore surely a matter of rejoicing to the Enlightenment.

There is reason to believe that D'Alembert's view was much more representative of Enlightenment opinion on that matter than was Voltaire's. Certainly the current of French opinion that descends from the Enlightenment—the *laïc* strain, in the nineteenth and twentieth centuries—although hostile to priests in general, was much more hostile to Jesuits in particular. So when the *laïcs* got the upper hand, in the first decade of the twentieth century, they expelled the Jesuits all over again.

Other priests were seen as benighted fellow countrymen, but at any rate fellow countrymen. Jesuits, with their special oath to the Pope, were seen as servants of a foreign power, which they attempted to set above *la nation.* So French Jesuits were not merely dispensers of superstition, but traitors to France, which was infinitely worse, indeed the worst thing possible. Looked at in that light, the twentieth-century laïcs were much less close to Voltaire than they were to the militant Gallican nationalism of the Jansenists.

I am interested in things that get filtered out of accepted history. One thing that got filtered out to a large extent in conventional retrospect on the prehistory of the French Revolution was Jansenist power: puritan and nationalist power. That the Jansenists did have power in late-eighteenth-century France had been spectacularly demonstrated in the matter of the Jesuits. In a more general way, throughout the period they remained a power within the parlements. And it was the King's otherwise insuperable difficulties with the parlements over taxation that drove Louis XVI to the desperate expedient of summoning the States-General, thereby setting in motion the revolutionary political process.

It would be wrong to attribute the King's difficulties with his parlements wholly or mainly to Jansenists. But he could not have been helped in his efforts to reach agreements with the parlements by the presence within them of a weighty and rancorous body of opinion that regarded the monarchy as having compromised the sacred liberties of the Gallican church. Whatever about the even larger matters, there is no question whatsoever about the role of the Jansenists in the sizable and significant matter that was the expulsion of the Jesuits. No contemporary was in any doubt about that. But, in retrospect, the people who did most to filter out the Jansenists were the Jesuits themselves, after the Restoration. The Jansenists may have expelled the Jesuits from France in the eighteenth century, but in the nineteenth century the Jesuits took revenge, by expelling the Jansenists from history.

The Jesuits, restored by the Restoration, insisted that the people responsible for their expulsion had been the philosophes. Jansenists? Who were they? Snobbery probably entered into this. The late-eighteenth-century Jansenists were a pretty weird lot, anomalous and eminently unfashionable, creatures out of one century astray in the next, animated fossils. And, to go around complaining that you have been bitten by a coelacanth is likely to excite curiosity rather than sympathy.

On the other hand, to present oneself as the victim of the redoubtable philosophes was, in the conditions of the Restoration, a passport to general sympathy. A lesson went along with it. The Jesuits, pedagogues to a man, were great ones for the lessons of history, even if the history had to be manipulated a bit to make room for the lessons. The lesson in this case was that the same evil godless forces that had deposed and decapitated Louis XVI had begun by expelling the Jesuits. Addressed to the monarchy, it ran: better hang on to the Jesuits, if you want to hang on to your head.

As it happened, the other side had no interest in discrediting this particular Jesuit distortion. If the philosophes had got the Jesuits thrown out, why then, good for the philosophes. The "all one struggle" idea suited both sides. As for the

Jansenists, who needed them? They had become "irrele-vant"—to use a term adopted by a later generation of students in order to filter out any and every aspect of reality which they found inconvenient.

Historiography took another beating at the hands of history. And insofar as the Jansenists were filtered out, with them went the most conspicuous manifestation, in the events leading up to the French Revolution, of the power of their puritan form of nationalism: extraneous to the Enlightenment, but in partial, awkward, and uncomfortable alliance with it. It is that filtering process which makes the origins of the French Revolution appear more alien to those of the American Revolution than was actually the case.

It took me some time to realize that there was *any* nationalism in the Enlightenment. When I began to study history, I used to think of the French Revolution as a curious contrivance, something like a turbine. In at one end poured a broad and placid stream of universalism, while what came out at the other end, for no visible reason, was a turbulent torrent of militant nationalism. Later, when I came to look a little closer at that first inward-flowing stream, I could see that under the universalist surface there was a great deal of nationalism in its composition.

In the earliest of the seminal documents of the Enlightenment, Spinoza's *Tractatus Theologico-Politicus,* published anonymously in Amsterdam in 1670, nationalism is emphatically articulate. In chapter III of the *Tractatus,* "De Vocatione Iudaeorum," Spinoza holds that the Jews were the Chosen People only as long as they complied with the rules their leaders had devised for them and kept their state in being: "Their election and vocation consisted solely in the temporal prosperity and advantages of their state. When through their own folly they lost their state and their land they ceased to be the Chosen People." He adds, quite consistently, but astonishingly: "Did not the principles of their religion make them effeminate, I should be quite convinced that one day when opportunity arises—so mutable are human affairs—they will establish their state once more and that God will choose them afresh."

More than 270 years later David Ben-Gurion, first Prime Minister of Israel, appealed to the rabbinate to revoke the sentence of excommunication passed by the Jewish religious authorities of Amsterdam in 1656 against Baruch Spinoza. In making that appeal, Ben-Gurion, in his turn, was entirely consistent. Is it not clear that the great philosopher had been a proto-Zionist—a nationalist of both the ancient and the modern type, within new intellectual structures largely of his own devising?

Thus, the principle of the transcendent rights of the nation-state, which may appear as a surprise in the revolutionary denouement of the Enlightenment, was present at its very beginning, in the greatest and most original mind of the whole process.

Spinoza comes very close to asserting the identity of nationalism and true religion when, in chapter XIX of the *Tractatus,* he says: "There is no doubt that devotion to country is the highest form of piety a man can show; for once the state is destroyed nothing good can survive." Here is the inherent tendency of the Enlightenment to exalt the nation-state. The Enlightenment removes a personal God, object of fear and love. It delegitimizes kingship, by desacralizing it. What is left? In theory, humanity is left. But humanity is at best a colorless abstraction. For most minds, and most nervous systems, penetrated by the Enlightenment, there was nothing left but the people—a particular people in a particular land, together with which it constituted the nation. The idea of a deified nation begins to beckon.

After Spinoza, the two writers who did most to develop the nationalist potential within the Enlightenment were Herder and Rousseau, in the second half of the eighteenth century. It may be significant that of the three prophets of nationalism within the Enlightenment, none was French and none belonged to the Catholic tradition. Spinoza was a Jew and, though a dissident, still steeped in Judaism. Herder belonged to the German Lutheran pietist subculture. Rousseau was born and brought up in Calvinist Geneva. All three were closer to the Old Testament, and less disposed to be funny about it, than were most Frenchmen of the Enlightenment. And all three worshiped something they called Nature, which was the mother of nations.

Rousseau's great achievement was to "fix" the emotional loyalties formerly associated with religion and now displaced. He diverted these loyalties toward the nation and exalted it into an absolute, in *The Social Contract,* through the concept of The General Will. He employed a median term, a bridge-word, over which the transferring loyalties passed. The bridge-word was virtue, *la vertu,* a word which Rousseau's literary genius, amid the cerebral aridities of the Enlightenment, turned into a source of tearful joy.

La vertu was an exquisitely well-chosen word, linking as it did what remained of the old religious ethic to the classical and Renaissance ideas of patriotism and martial valor: *virtus, virtù.* Rousseau's most fervent and energetic disciple was Robespierre, who defined *la vertu* as consisting of "the love of the good, of *la patrie* and of liberty." That was in 1792; in the following year, if Robespierre discerned in any person a deficiency of *la vertu,* that person was promptly decapitated.

And Robespierre was not alone. The entire Revolution was dominated by the exalted Rousseauistic concept of the nation. In 1789 the Abbe Sieyes, in his seminal pamphlet "What Is the Third Estate?" wrote: "The nation exists before all, it is the origin of everything. Its will is always legal, it is the law itself."

"God Land" indeed, under the colors of the social contract. Jules Michelet, heir and historian of the French Revolution, left moving testimony of his own personal need for a nation—God: "It is from you that I shall ask for help, my noble country: you must take the place of the God who escapes us [le dieu qui nous echappe], that you may fill within us the immeasurable abyss which extinct Christianity [le christianisme eteint] has left there."

Jean-Jacques Rousseau, "citizen of Geneva," was not a French nationalist. But he liberated the demon of French nationalism, as well as of other nationalisms. Herder was not himself a daimonic character; he detested Prussian militarism, and therefore was far from being what later generations would think of as a typical German nationalist. But later and more militant, Prussianizing, German nationalists, like Fichte, were grateful to Herder for teaching nationalism to Germans. They were prepared to overlook, or rather to filter out, his pacific and anti-Prussian deviations.

Herder, the high priest of cultural nationalism, rejected the cultural hegemony of Paris with the same fervor that his forebears had used in rejecting the religious hegemony of Rome. He regretted that Luther had not founded a national church for the German people, and his own writings may be seen as an effort to fill that void with a cult of the German language, the German land, and the "national soul." Herder is strong in holy geography; landscape is invested with a specifically national aura. Of a walk in the Teutoburger Wald, he writes: "I am now in the country, in the most beautiful, the most rugged, the most German, the most romantic region in the world." With Herder begins a sort of tic that afflicts all later nationalist writers. This is the need to prefix the word "national" to any and every phenomenon or practice that is deemed desirable. Wherever that tic appears, nationalism is on a high, and it is well to watch out.

Just as Herder detested Prussian militarism, so Frederick the Great despised German nationalism. But the ill-assorted pair became part of an ominous Valhalla, which both would have disliked, for different reasons, but which both had helped to construct.

The climacteric year with regard to the genesis of the two great eighteenth-century revolutions is 1763: the year of the Treaty of Paris and the end of the Seven Years' War.

After 1763 nationalism speeds up and becomes more exalted, for different but related reasons, in France, in Germany, and in America.

In France the stimulus was national humiliation, with the
need to restore national pride.

In Germany the stimulus was restoration of national pride
after long humiliation.

In America the stimulus was the removal of a danger, that
of the French power in North America, which had long served
to bind the English-speaking colonies to their metropolis.

□

How did religion and nationalism interact in America in this
decisive period between the end of the Seven Years' War and
the outbreak of the Revolution?

To use a somewhat flamboyant metaphor, there are similar,
but not identical, politico-religious constellations blazing in
the skies of France and of America. Both are triangles and in
both the stars are the same: Religion, Enlightenment, Nationalism. But the stars do not stand in the same relation to one
another; the triangles are of different types.

In France supernatural religion was far gone in decline, and
the emotions formerly attached to the supernatural were being
displaced onto the new terrestrial religion of nationalism. In
America supernatural religion remained vigorous, versatile,
and dynamic in a multiplicity of Protestant forms. The Enlightenment strongly affected the mind of an elite, especially
the rising political leadership, but the American Enlightenment was not hostile to Protestantism in the way that the
French Enlightenment was to Catholicism.

What the American and French Enlightenments had in
common was a hostility, not to religion in general, but
specifically to Roman Catholicism. In America a common
hostility to Roman Catholicism was a powerful bonding force,
both between Enlightenment people and fundamentalist Protestants and also between Protestants of different theological
opinions and different degrees of religious intensity—New
Lights, Old Lights, and so on.

Up to the 1760s what one might call pan-Protestantism had

been another bonding force between the colonies and Great Britain. True, American Calvinists regarded the Anglican establishment with considerable suspicion. But the Anglican establishment was not Great Britain. Arminianism might be established in that entity which Calvinists liked to refer to as "the southern part of Great Britain," but Calvinism was established in Scotland. The British monarch, head of the Churches of England and Scotland, is a theological schizophrenic.

More important than those oddities was the fact that British Protestants of all descriptions, including American Britons, could take pride in being part of the mightiest Protestant power on earth. They could, that is, up to the 1760s. From 1763 on, and much more consistently after 1765, Americans were asking themselves whether Great Britain was Protestant at all.

They had not been disposed to press that question before 1763. Until then the British and the colonists had a common Roman Catholic enemy: the French in Canada. Many of the colonists from 1745 to 1763 had seen the struggle with the French in terms of the millennial hopes present from the earliest settlements and fanned by the Great Awakening of the 1730s on. French Canada was "the North American Babylon"; the conflict over it, Armageddon; invasion of Canada, the "grand decisive conflict between the Lamb and beast." It followed that exalted millennial hopes attended on the idea of the eventual decisive victory over the French in Canada. It was predicted that the fall of French Canada would bring "a most signal revolution in the civil and religious state of the world," nothing less than "the accomplishment of the scripture prophecy relative to the Millennial State."

The decisive victory of 1763, with the British acquisition of French Canada, could neither satisfy these millennial hopes nor dispel them. The victory exalted the hopes, but the British conduct of the victory frustrated them. After 1763 the British did not behave at all like partners with the colonists in a millennial achievement. On the contrary, they seemed to be bent on conciliation of the old Romish enemy and perhaps on betraying the Protestant colonists who had borne so much of the burden of the war.

The British had agreed, in the peace treaty with France, to allow their King's "new Roman Catholic subjects . . . the worship of their religion according to the rites of the Romish Church." They had provided for a papist bishop up there in Canada (1766–67). At the same time, and perhaps by no coincidence, they and their warmest admirers in North America, the Episcopalians of the Middle Colonies, were talking about bringing Anglican bishops to the English-speaking colonies. Might not all this be part of some sinister Grand Design for the imposition of a papist or semipapist system in America?

The idea of a Grand Design would not have been credible on such slight evidence had it not been for the climate of aroused and frustrated millennial expectations among the disaffected colonists. In that climate the idea was widely credible, and it helped to turn those expectations into a new channel. The expected "signal revolution in the civil and religious state of the world" was to take the specific form of a political revolution against the British Crown.

It wasn't entirely a matter of millennial expectations. There was the basic politico-military fact that, with the elimination of French power in North America, the colonists no longer needed the British. The colonists wanted to stand on their own feet and be master in their own house. But they also felt that that wish was in accordance with God's plan for America. It could be said that the colonists were in quest of a religious sanction for a political challenge to Britain. But the colonists themselves seem to have considered their political rights and the cause of their religion inseparably intertwined.

In 1765 the Stamp Act, as interpreted in many of the colonies' pulpits, appeared like an attack not only on political rights, but also on religious freedom. John Adams explains the religious aspect of the Stamp Act as it appeared to the colonists: "It was known that neither king, nor ministry, nor archbishops, could appoint bishops in America without an act of Parliament and if Parliament could tax us, they could establish the Church of England, with all its creeds, articles, tests, ceremonies, and titles, and prohibit all other churches as conventicles and schism shops."

"No stamping, no episcopizing" became an effective slogan, welding the secular and the religious causes into one. As Carl Bridenbaugh puts it: "Religion and politics could never again be distinguished from one another after the uproar created in the Colonies by the Stamp Act."

Alan Heimert develops the theme: "The decade that began with the Stamp Act crisis and culminated in the battle of Lexington was thus distinguished by something far more impressive than the mere application of religious doctrine to politics. The very religious life of the colonies came to center on the crisis in public affairs, and, indeed, to be defined by it and from it to derive vitality." I shall come back to this very significant statement.

The repeal of the Stamp Act, in 1766, did not cause the religious-political uproar to subside. The British Parliament, though repealing that specific Act, in a Declaratory Act reasserted Parliament's "power and authority to bind the Colonies and people of America subject to the Crown of Great Britain." So the combined threat to political freedom and freedom of religion remained suspended over the colonists, and the agitation continued to increase.

If the unrest in the colonies had been concentrated on economic and fiscal grievances, the repeal of the Stamp Act might have ended it. But the unrest was far wider and deeper, drawing on religious as well as political sources. The defeat of the Stamp Act was celebrated as a victory, but an incomplete one as long as the British Parliament continued to claim a *right* to tax the colonists. The Declaratory Act, by reason of the very fact that it was a declaration of principle, was a more direct challenge to emerging revolutionary feeling, both political and religious, than the Stamp Act had been. Failure to see this may have been the great flaw in Edmund Burke's otherwise impressive American policy. The range of Burke's intellect and imagination might have allowed him, more than any other British politician, to comprehend the gravity of a crisis in which religion and politics were converging. And he did understand the gravity of the crisis better than any other parliamentarian of the period. Yet in his public statements he seems no more aware than his more prosaic contemporaries—and some historians since—that there was any religious dimension to the crisis.

There may have been a personal reason why Burke did not want to face this aspect. In a general way, he was sympathetic to the colonists. But the religious aspect of their agitation, with its strong charge of antipopery, could only be profoundly distasteful to Burke, with his Irish Catholic family background and lifelong commitment to Catholic emancipation. So it is understandable that he might not have wished to listen to the pulpits of New England in the decade before the American Revolution.

Yet even if he had listened to them—and perhaps he did—there was no way he could have conveyed their message to any Parliament of George III's. He would have had to say, in substance: "When you assert your right to 'bind' the colonists, many of them see you as trying to frustrate God's design for America and to postpone the millennium." Many of Burke's contemporaries already thought him odd enough; if he had attempted to deliver any such message as that, he would have been thought fit for Bedlam. By 1766 the British Parliament and the disaffected colonists had become mutually unintelligible. In those conditions Burke may well have felt that to get the Stamp Act repealed, on strictly pragmatic grounds, at the price of the face-saving Declaratory Act was the best that could be done. He knew that it might not be enough.

In the later phases of the prerevolutionary agitation, the religious theme became more and more insistent. In late 1774 it came to an almost frenzied crescendo with the passage of the Quebec Act, at Westminster, on the eve of the convening of the First Continental Congress. The Quebec Act was seen as proof that the Grand Design—the two-pronged attack from Britain on the religious and political freedoms of Americans—was being put into execution. The Act, which might have seemed innocuous enough to people not in the grip of revolutionary excitement, was seen as simultaneously confirming an alliance between the British Crown with the Canadian papists and as closing the doors of the West to Protestant emigration. The Protestant colonies were encompassed and confined by a British-and-papist alliance, whose next objective would be the destruction of Protestantism in America.

This phase is distinguished by the intensity, exuberance, and abundance of its antipopery rhetoric. Anyone who may doubt that statement should inspect the copious evidence assembled in Charles Metzger's *The Quebec Act*. Antipopery had arrived in North America along with the first colonists, and the strength of popery in the mother country had been a recurring theme there at intervals ever since. The theme had been present, in relatively subdued forms, in earlier phases of the agitation, but in 1774–75, for a brief but crucial period it drowns out every other theme in the preparation for the Revolution. It was an element that was filtered out in a number of later retrospects on the period, but it was abundantly there and it served a serious purpose.

Essentially what the preachers, the secular orators, the journalists, and the cartoonists who beat the antipopery drum at this time were saying was: "The Quebec Act proves what we have been suspecting for years: the British King is in collusion with papists and is little better than a papist himself. Wake up, remember what a frightful thing popery is and how your ancestors felt about it, and then you will be able to defend your liberties, religious and civil." It proved a highly effective method of arousing and mobilizing revolutionary energies.

The American religious and political agitation, from 1763 to 1775 was, as far as I know, the most formidable and most momentous manifestation of holy nationalism that ever occurred anywhere. But how holy was the nationalism? How nationalistic the holiness? Which provides the driving force: the religion or the politics?

The American Tories, who had to bear the brunt both of the agitation and of its revolutionary consequences, had definite views on all that. For them, the "black regiment" of Calvinist divines were political agitators in clerical dress. The entire agitation was essentially political in its motivation and its objectives. Religion was being ransacked to provide texts and pretexts to serve political ends and to inflame the mob. (During the Revolution, British Army officers took the same view as they burned down Calvinist places of worship. Unlike British politicians—and some historians—the Army had to take some account of the religious aspects of the Revolution: "Profanation of religion," General Burgoyne called them.)

Obviously the Tories had a case. And the course of the Revolution seemed to offer confirmation of it. Hypocrisy in the use of religion appeared as blatant in certain addresses of the Continental Congress in October 1774. On October 21 the Congress released an "Address to the People of Great Britain," condemning Parliament for establishing in Canada a religion which had deluged England with blood and "disbursed impiety, bigotry, persecution, murder and rebellion through every part of the world." Five days later this same Congress issued an "Address to the Inhabitants of the Province of Quebec," in which the totally papist addressees were alleged to be too fully cognizant of the "liberality of sentiment" prevailing among the English-speaking colonists to suppose that a difference in religion would prevent a hearty friendship between the two peoples.

A decade later John Adams declared that the people revered the Congress as "the voice of God." In October 1774 God could be heard to contradict himself.

George Washington himself was concerned about the excesses of holy nationalism. On November 5, 1775, shortly after assuming office as Commander-in-Chief, in his orders for the abolition of "Pope Day," he condemned "that ridiculous and childish custom of burning the effigy of the Pope." Washington was temperamentally and philosophically averse from all such goings-on. But, as the text of those orders shows, he was also aware of how profoundly inopportune such displays of antipopery were, granted the political and strategic necessities and possibilities of the Revolution.

A few years later came the alliance with His Most Christian Majesty of France, who was allied with His Most Catholic Majesty of Spain. The contemporary American variety of holy nationalism had to be put into cold storage for the duration. It is during this period that you have John Adams attending High Mass. (Poor old George III at least never did *that!*) And then, after Yorktown, that French *Te Deum* in Philadelphia brought to a decorous and ecumenical close an agenda which had begun, less than ten years before, with an orgy of antipopery.

We note that, *after* the Revolution the United States extended exactly the same tolerance to papists that the British, *before* the Revolution, had been denounced for extending in Canada.

It is easy to be cynical about all this, but some cynicism is surely in order. At the same time, the religious enthusiasm that accompanied the movement toward revolution was deep and genuine; even if some of it may also have been deliberately stimulated by politicians who were not necessarily religious themselves. The culture, after all, was so saturated with religion that a political crisis—a moment of fateful choice—had to be experienced by many as a religious crisis as well.

As John Adams indicated, from the beginning religion and politics had been associated in New England. And with the Great Awakening, in the first half of the eighteenth century, many Americans throughout the colonies had become convinced that in America, God was preparing the millennium. To tamper with America, to stand in America's way, was to oppose God's will. That is how, in Heimert's words, the "religious life of the colonies came to center on the crisis in public affairs."

Manifestations of religious exaltation on the eve of the Revolution had a solemn and specific function: they constituted a ritual of passage from one allegiance to another, delegitimizing the old and legitimizing the new. The image of the Pope, jointly with that of George III, was essential to the working of the ritual. The Glorious Revolution of 1688 against a papist king was not merely a hallowed event in the eyes of Britons and Americans; it was the source of legitimacy itself. If George III could be shown to have betrayed the Glorious Revolution by his connivance with popery and his arbitrary acts, then George III was no legitimate sovereign. And he *was* so shown, in the prerevolutionary religious manifestations; so shown, that is, so depicted. In terms of the ritual, that sufficed. There was no need for evidence that would satisfy an impartial jury, if such existed. What was needed was to fill Americans, as they embarked on revolution, with a sense of the righteousness of their cause and a conviction that God was on their side. One can sense that the revolutionary preachers were convincing themselves as they went along, employing any argument that would serve to satisfy the spiritual-cum-political need of their congregations, a need which they, too, experienced.

After the Revolution, as before, antipopery continued to be an unofficial part of American life. But it would never again be as central and as essential as it had been during the prerevolutionary ritual of transition. The Pope, as Edmund Burke said about this time, is "a commodious bugbear."

Holy nationalism went into cold storage during the short period of the French and Spanish alliances; more precisely, it went into a phase of unaccustomed taciturnity. But once the revolutionary victory was complete, holy nationalism found its voice again and took many a bow. It was entitled to; it had played a vital part in the great transition.

□

Holy nationalism was a major factor in preparing the way for both the French and American Revolutions; but there is a large difference between the two types of holy nationalism. The history of the Great Seal of the United States is a striking example of the continuity of American holy nationalism, not only with that of the Old Testament and of classical antiquity but also with that of the European Middle Ages. The distribution of aspects of the continuity, as between the beginning of the Revolution, and its victorious outcome, is of particular interest.

The same day that the Congress agreed to the Declaration of Independence, July 4, 1776, it appointed Benjamin Franklin, John Adams, and Thomas Jefferson a Committee to devise a device for a seal of the United States of America. Both Franklin and Jefferson proposed Old Testament themes. Franklin's design showed "Moses standing on the shore and extending his hand over the Sea, thereby causing the same to overwhelm Pharaoh, who is sitting in an open Chariot, a Crown on his Head and a Sword in his Hand. Rays from the Pillar of Fire in the Clouds, reaching to Moses, to express that he acts by Command of the Deity"; the motto is REBELLION TO TYRANTS IS OBEDIENCE TO GOD. Jefferson proposed "the children of Israel in the wilderness, led by a cloud by day and a pillar of fire by night."

Neither the Franklin nor the Jefferson design was approved, and the matter apparently was left in abeyance as long as the issue of the Revolutionary war was in doubt. After Yorktown such matters could again receive attention, and on June 20, 1782, the Continental Congress adopted the Great Seal, in substantially its present form. This Seal is largely of classical inspiration, without any Old Testament themes; the words are in Latin. The Eagle in this context suggests continuity with ancient Rome, a continuity developed on the reverse of the seal. The motto ANNUIT COEPTIS (He has prospered our undertakings) is from the Aeneid. The motto INCIPIT NOVUS ORDO SAECLORUM (A new Order of the Ages begins) is also Virgilian, being derived from the Sibylline Prophecy of the Fourth Eclogue, which medieval Christianity had adopted as prefiguring the Christian era. Just as Constantine had applied the

Eclogue to his own Christian Empire, so the Founding Fathers applied it to the United States.

The seal was designed by then Secretary of Congress Charles Thomson, whose explanation of the reverse says: "The Pyramid signifies strength and duration. The eye over it and the motto allude to the many signal interventions of Providence in favour of the American cause."

It seems that, while the Old Testament was felt to provide satisfactory imagery and rhetoric for revolutionary war, the Roman heritage was deemed more appropriate to the official apparatus of the newborn United States. Yet throughout the nineteenth and into even the late twentieth century the Old Testament continued to provide symbolism for what Ronald Reagan, at the midpoint of his first presidential term, called "this anointed land."

Many modern Americans seem to think of American civilization as a distinctive growth out of American soil, almost a product of parthenogenesis, in a land set apart from the Old World not only by geography but by history. Yet the story of the design for the Great Seal shows the Founding Fathers as acutely conscious of America's roots in the Old World—not only in the British Isles, but in the ancient eastern and western Mediterranean.

The story of the Great Seal also has some bearing on that scale, considered in Chapter 2, of "chosen people," "holy nation," and "deified nation." The designs of Franklin and Jefferson were in line with the Puritanism of John Winthrop and William Bradford; of Richard, Increase, and Cotton Mather; of Thomas Hooker and many others. Americans were, in some sense, a chosen people. But a chosen people might well have to be punished, like the Jews, for breaches of the Covenant. Yet the design actually approved by the Continental Congress in June 1782 tended to move America from the conditional and therefore relatively chastened status of "chosen people" into the complacencies of "holy nation" and in the direction of "deified nation."

Rome was a goddess, and the Eternal City. The Caesars

were gods. No sins that Rome or Caesar could commit could change that. In opting for a Roman symbolism, rather than an Old Testament one, the Continental Congress was already showing a certain appetite for hubris.

□

In the same period America's ally France, under Rousseau's influence, was also developing a cult of Ancient Rome, part of a prerevolutionary process of incipient deification of the nation. Americans seem to have felt an urge to move in the same direction, but it was not as easy for them to do so as it was for the French. For many French people Christianity had become "extinct," as it had for Michelet. In America that had not happened. There was still a God, distinguishable—if at times only dimly—from the nation that was the object of His peculiar concern.

The French Revolution, fanned to some extent by "the wind from America," broke out seven years after the end of the American one.

French holy nationalism, as inherited from Rousseau by Sieyes and Robespierre, replaced supernatural religion with a cult of the nation. Sieyes acknowledged no entity or law superior to the nation. Robespierre actually did propose a cult of the Supreme Being, but it did not catch on. For most French Revolutionaries and their successors in that tradition the nation itself, with no superior, was the object of worshipful allegiance. Other purely secular nationalisms were to follow suit in other countries. All that belongs in the "deified nation" school of holy nationalism.

America, on the other hand, richly endowed with supernatural religion, could not possibly deify herself in that way. I say, "in that way," because there may be other ways. But the idea of America as a manifestation, or aspect, of the divine could sometimes come close to worship of a deified nation.

4

God Land Now

On Thursday, January 31, 1985, in the International Ballroom of the Washington Hilton Hotel, I attended the Thirty-Third Annual National Prayer Breakfast, organized by members of the United States Senate and the House of Representatives. On the platform were the President of the United States and Mrs. Reagan; Vice-President and Mrs. Bush; Secretary of State George Shultz; senators and representatives; Sandra Day O'Connor of the U.S. Supreme Court; the Chief of Staff of the United States Army, General John A. Wickham, Jr.; the Governor of California and the Mayor of Philadelphia; and a number of other notables.

Coffee was served immediately after the entry of the President and the First Lady. Then the presiding officer, the Honorable Ralph Regula (U.S. Representative, Ohio), chairman of the House Prayer Breakfast Committee, was on his feet. The Congressman hit the keynote, with a loud bang. He prayed aloud to God the Father. I took down his words—the Congressman's, that is—and what he said was this: "In the excitement of the presence of the President of the United States of America, help us to remember the presence of Your Son, Jesus Christ." I looked round at my neighbors, but none of them seemed to find anything incongruous about the idea that Reagan might upstage Jesus, unless the Father threw His weight into the balance.

At the time I found Mr. Regula's words mind-boggling. Reflecting on the matter later, however, in the general context of this book's subject, I found some positive significance in what I shall call the Regula Invocation. That Invocation now seems to me expressive of a conflict, within what contemporary sociologists call "the American civil religion," between the nationalist and the supernatural components. The Congressman's words represented an effort not to be altogether swept away by a powerful current moving in the direction of a cult of the deified nation, incarnate in the President. So I can now see something touching and benign in tendency, however feebly so, in a phenomenon that once appeared merely bizarre and absurd: the Regula Invocation.

There is something rather mysterious about the peculiarly American institution of the Annual National Prayer Breakfast. What is mysterious is that it does not seem to attract public attention to a degree even remotely proportionate to its apparent significance. Here we have a national assemblage in the nation's capital: an assembly instituted by a president and annually participated in by presidents and leading representatives of both houses of Congress, of the Supreme Court, and of the Armed Forces, as well as by governors of great states and mayors of great cities, and by thousands of Americans from all over the country. You might think a phenomenon of that order would attract quite an amount of public as well as of scholarly interest. Yet it does not seem to do so.

The National Prayer Breakfast is now nearly thirty-five years old. It was begun by President Eisenhower in 1953, at the beginning of his first term, and has taken place every year since then, under every presidency and with the participation of every president.

Yet many otherwise well-informed Americans have never heard of the National Prayer Breakfast. Officially, the very existence of the thing hardly seems to be acknowledged. The great American newspaper of record ignores its existence; I have searched the *New York Times* index for mention of it, but in vain. Nor does the scholarly world seem to be agog. That generally admirable learned periodical, the *Journal for the Scientific Study of Religion,* has rightly given much attention since the 1960s to the question of the American civil religion as expressed in Independence Day, Memorial Day, and so on. Yet I can find nothing about what appears a highly significant annual manifestation of the civil religion—the National Prayer Breakfast, led by the highest officers of the Constitution, and bringing the profession of supernatural religion into closer association with the political structure than the spirit of the Constitution seems to encourage. Puzzled by the "information gap" around this interesting politico-religious phenomenon, I made some inquiries in Washington. My friend Walter Reich, of the Wilson Center for the Study of Democratic Institutions, put me in touch with Gerald A. Franz, Arrangements Coordinator of the National Prayer Breakfast. Mr. Franz's courteous reply to my inquiries did provide a clue of sorts to the low profile of these high-level proceedings: "The National Prayer Breakfast is an event sponsored by the Senate Prayer Group and the House of Representatives Prayer Groups and it has been their wish to keep it informal and worshipful so not much historical information has been retained."

The briefing (supplied to me by Mr. Franz) for the 1987 National Prayer Breakfast makes it clear that "National" in this context embraces only American Christians, for the Breakfast celebrates "a common commitment to Christ" and "friendship in Christ."

I wonder whether a certain uneasiness about the compatibility of all this with the separation of Church and State may underlie the apparent reluctance of the media and the scholarly world to scrutinize the phenomenon. Certainly to the candid eye the National Prayer Breakfast does not suggest a separation of Church and State. Rather, it appears to be the State engaged in a collective act of Christian worship. A visitor who could judge only by the National Prayer Breakfast would think that the United States had an established religion, pan-Christian and pan-Trinitarian.

The National Prayer Breakfast seems to have a specific and

practical function. Instituted by a military president, and annually timed for a critical period in the fiscal year of the United States, the Breakfast apparently is there to call down God's blessing on the military budget and to mobilize Christian support for the same through the various Christian fellowships whose members make up the bulk of the audience/congregation. On the occasion that I attended, the point was made with memorable clarity in the Closing Prayer delivered by General Wickham. It ran: "Oh Lord, help us defend our freedom. Freedom is never free. It is the most expensive thing on earth. And it must be paid for in installments."

In April 1987, again in Washington, I had another, and to me more disturbing encounter with what is generally called the American civil religion. I prefer to call it "national religion" because I think that term better evokes the collective emotions underlying such phenomena. The phenomenon I encountered that day is a national shrine known as the Air and Space Museum.

The Air and Space Museum is, I am told, the most visited museum on earth. I am sure it is a jolly place in the daytime, when it is full of young people enjoying a kind of cosmic Disneyland. But I visited it in the middle of the night, when nobody was there but uniformed guardians. So visited, the Museum of Air and Space can make a chilling impression; at least it did on me.

I seemed to be in a huge, coldly cavernous cathedral dedicated to the glory of the United States, coextensive with the cosmos. Two verses from the Gospel according to Saint Luke came unbidden to my mind: "And the devil, taking him up into a high mountain, shewed unto him all the kingdoms of the world in a moment of time. And the devil said unto him, All this power will I give thee, and the glory of them: for that is delivered unto me; and to whomsoever I will I give it" (4:5–6). I tried to hear America say "Get thee behind me, Satan," but I heard nothing just then. Instead we have Star Wars, of which Garry Wills writes: "What is Star Wars but another more complex projector meant to trace, in lasers and benign nuclear 'searchlighting,' the image of America itself, across the widest screen of all."

Earlier in this book I distinguished three kinds of holy nationalism, with "chosen people" as a relatively moderate kind, "deified nation" as the extreme, and "holy nation" in the middle. During the last six years or so the needle of holy nationalism in the United States seems to have been hovering somewhere between "holy nation" and "deified nation." The National Prayer Breakfast was "holy nation" stuff. As one speaker, the then Governor of California, put it: "without God there could be no America. This sacred American compact with God." At that level God and America remain distinguishable entities. But in the Museum of Air and Space the distinction vanishes. The only God in that cosmogony is the United States.

A lot has been said about the danger of the religious right and that particular manifestation of holy nationalism. I am by no means attracted to the religious right, and I am uncomfortable with even the more mildly nationalistic climate of the Prayer Breakfast culture. Nevertheless, were the United States a less religious country in the ordinary or God-fearing sense, I think American nationalism would be more dangerous than it is. I am less afraid of an alliance between nationalism and religion than I am of a fusion of nationalism and technology, claiming not merely the earth but the heavens as well and clothing the nation with the omnipotence of God. In a word, I am less afraid of the National Prayer Breakfast than I am of the Museum of Air and Space.

Religion at least attempts to place certain inhibitions on the destructive potential of nationalism. The attempts are often diffident, the inhibitions fragile; still, they are better than nothing. In the fusion of nationalism and technology, on the other hand, the technology is unreservedly at the service of the nationalism. The system contains within it no inhibiting factors. It is a triumphalist version of science fiction. "The force is with us!" exclaimed President Reagan apropos of his own Strategic Defense Initiative. In the same context he invoked the image of Superman. Not, I think, Friedrich Nietzsche's Superman. Perhaps we should be grateful for that small mercy.

The level of hubris in the American atmosphere had become disturbingly high by 1986. After November of that year the hubris level seemed to drop significantly. A limited misfortune may turn out to be a piece of good fortune in relative terms. It can make you pause and reconsider, instead of continuing to hurtle forward on a path that might lead you even deeper into trouble. So may it prove with Irangate.

In the late twentieth century nationalisms often wear masks and fool one another, in a curious game of blindman's buff. Take the case of Nicaragua. No one who has any feeling for nationalism can spend any time in that country without being aware that nationalism is a driving force behind the reigning political ideology, Sandinismo. The eponymous hero of the movement, Augusto César Sandino, is the classical hero and martyr of a national liberation struggle, and there is a national cult of heroes and martyrs, from him down to the latest victim of the Contras. The Contras and their friends are seen as *vendepatrias,* people who sell their country, the epithet that Sandino applied to his enemies and which remains the greatest stigma in the vocabulary of the Sandinistas. The Sandinista motto, Sandino's own, is quintessentially nationalist: *patria libre o morir.*

Yet the reigning wisdom in the United States is that the Sandinistas are not really nationalists at all. They, or at least their leaders, are crafty Marxist-Leninists whose real loyalty is not to Nicaragua but to the Soviet Union. According to this view, it is for the benefit of the Soviet Union that the Sandinistas manipulate the vocabulary of nationalism as well as that of liberation theology.

After a visit to Nicaragua early in 1986 I reported that, in my view, Sandinismo is essentially a nationalist movement with a Marxist-Leninist component, the latter being encroached upon by liberation theology, more congenial than Marxism-Leninism to the Latin culture. Latin American nationalism and liberation theology blend in a recognizable form of holy nationalism comparable to that of the early Puritans.

Predictably this account was badly received by dispensers of the reigning wisdom. These are in general tidy-minded people, whose concepts are arranged in firmly separated compartments, with none of the slipperiness of the ideas we have been examining. For such tidy-minded people Marxism-Leninism and nationalism are, quite simply, incompatible. If someone who is on record as professing Marxism-Leninism carries on like a nationalist, he must be trying to fool people.

What I find most disturbing about the tidy-minded ones is that they seem incapable of learning from experience. In the 1950s they used to carry on about the Sino-Soviet bloc. If told the Chinese Communists were also Chinese nationalists, they smiled the superior smile of those who know that such things cannot be. And even after the breach between China and the Soviet Union demonstrated, in an earth-shaking manner, that these people had been quite wrong, they continued to reason exactly as before. They knew that the Vietcong could not be nationalists. And they know the same about the Sandinistas today.

What these people think they know makes them expensive guides to a political world that is by no means as tidily constructed as they continue to assume.

Look at the Marxist side of the picture. Marxists can be seen as a kind of Chosen People, visible saints of a terrestrial religion. The god who chose them is called History, and his covenant with them is set out in *Das Kapital*. Their Promised Land is the entire world. But for them, too, the millennium does not in fact dawn. They, too, have to make do with bits of land and bits of history and reinterpret their covenant in the light of local and temporal realities.

In the Soviet Union today Marxism-Leninism—more accurately by now, Leninism—appears less a revolutionary creed than a national or civil religion, with established modes of discourse and ceremonial, holding together a strange assortment of peoples.

In the Soviet Union, as in the America of Solomon Stoddard, visible saints turned into a holy nation. Soviet society is not an overall success story, but Soviet nationalism—multinational nationalism—has been far more successful than is commonly recognized. Soviet nationalism is largely the creation of the genius of Joseph Stalin, who interpreted the national question for Lenin and made good his interpretation. Stalin, backed by Lenin, achieved the extraordinary feat during the civil war years of bringing together again almost all the lands of the former Russian Empire. This was accomplished not solely by force of arms and manipulations of factions—though both entered into it—but also by the power of an idea: an international idea. The Whites in the civil war were offering, to Tadjiks and Uzbeks and so on, specifically *Russian* things: restoration of the tsardom and the Russian Orthodox Church. Lenin and Stalin offered cultural autonomy, with an ostensibly international ideology and an ostensibly international union. To the ambitious, they offered a share in the power of an ostensibly international elite, the Communist Party. It worked. In a multitude of local conflicts, the Bolshevik factions prevailed.

In theory, all this was part of a general process of world revolution. In practice, it culminated in Soviet nationalism, which successfully combined differentiated cultural nationalisms with one overriding political nationalism. What is important about Marxism within this system is not that it is believed to be universally valid but that it is the national religion of the Soviet Union. Just as what was important about Orthodoxy was not its doctrinal peculiarities but the fact that it was the national religion of Holy Russia. Central to the modern Soviet religion is the cult of the fallen in the Great Patriotic War. Pericles would have understood this perfectly.

Nevertheless, the continuing theoretical commitment of the Soviet Union to world revolution has certain practical implications, though these appear to be more limited than is sometimes supposed. All public and semipublic political debates in the Soviet Union at every level have to be conducted in the language and according to the concepts of Marxism-Leninism, irrespective of whether the speaker does or does not believe them. Indeed it may be that the word "belief" is no longer appropriate. We do not think of ourselves as believing in English, if it's the language we speak; we just speak it. I suspect that Soviet citizens speak Marxism in very much the same way. If that is the way you have to speak, you'd better believe it.

In any case, Soviet citizens appear capable of believing simultaneously in the things they are taught at school and in other things, picked up elsewhere, which belong in a different world from that of school. The British anthropologist Caroline Humphrey offers a splendid example of this in her book *Karl Marx Collective*. The farmers of the Karl Marx Collective on Lake Baikal are good Marxists; at the same time they are good Siberian Shamanists. They are taught at school to venerate the martyrs of the Paris Commune of 1871. And indeed those farmers *do* venerate those martyrs! Humphrey describes the form their veneration takes:

> The farmers worship the communist Uhan-Khaalyuud ("water otters"), a god or perhaps a group of gods, which lives in Lake Baikal and is the metamorphosis of the Parisian communards who were defeated in 1871. They took refuge in Lake Baikal, underwent metamorphosis into otters, and now, if sacrifices are made to them, they give help with the fulfilling of the plan (in this case, with the plan for fish). Sacrifices are made both by individuals and by the collectivity at the end of May and beginning of June when the fishing season starts.

Nor is the worship of the communard otters by the Soviet collective farmers an isolated anomaly within the Soviet society. It is part of a general pattern, recognized by Soviet ethnographers, which helps to hold Soviet Siberia together. The Buryat ethnographer T. M. Mikhailov writes:

From conversations with Buryat shamans which I carried out in 1960–3, I was able to distinguish a particular shamanist ideology. Everything which occurs in the world, they maintain, is the doing of supernatural forces. The October socialist revolution, Soviet power, the building of Communism, etc., all this is the will of the gods. The Communists are their emissaries to the earth. Lenin, Sverdlov, Kalinin—in a word all the main figures of the CP, USSR and the Soviet state—are also deities, which, together with the sky gods (tengri) and "kings of nature" (Khat), hold meetings in the other world and decide about matters which are important to living people. The shamanist religion thus helps Soviet power.

On our tripartite scale of holy nationalism I would rank the Soviet society somewhat between "chosen people" and "holy nation." The Soviet god, History, has visited his people with the most terrible suffering during as well as between the two World Wars. Soviet people fear that it may happen again and that there are Americans who want to make it happen. "Star Wars" is something of a joke to many Americans. To the Soviet people it is no joke but a set of technological innovations intended to make it possible for the Soviet Union to be attacked with impunity.

I do not mean to make an unfair contrast between an American nationalism aflame with hubris and a Soviet nationalism which is peaceable and defensive. I do believe that at present there is more hubris in American nationalism than there is in the Soviet kind. Americans, after all, have more to feel hubris about. But hubris has been manifest in Soviet nationalism under Stalin and under Khrushchev. That of the immediate postsputnik period was particularly dangerous, with Khrushchev promising to bury the United States and then secretly planting missiles in Cuba. It was Soviet hubris that brought the world, in 1962, into the most dangerous crisis experienced since the end of the Second World War. Since then, however, the hubris component in Soviet nationalism appears to have declined significantly, while the equivalent component in American nationalism has fluctuated at relatively high levels and, since 1980, has become disturbingly conspicuous.

Still, there remains an apparently huge potential for hubris in the Soviet ideology, or national religion. World revolution is the Soviet version of "manifest destiny," and a commitment to world revolution is a central element of the official religion—something that was not true of American "manifest destiny." This official or religious commitment of the Soviet system does have a significant influence on world affairs, though not as momentous an influence as is sometimes attributed to it.

I do not accept the theories of Jean-François Revel and others that the Soviet Union is forever working on some vast master plan for revolution throughout the Third World, preparing the way for revolution in the industrialized countries. I think the processes at work are much more spontaneous, piecemeal, and erratic than any such schemas suggest. And the impetus is supplied much more by forces in the Third World itself than by the Kremlin.

□

Marxism has a strong appeal in Third World countries, *precisely to nationalists*. The appeal is multifaceted. To begin with, the Third World nationalist feels that his country is being, or has been, or is in danger of being, humiliated and exploited by international capitalism, or one particular capitalist country. The nationalist generally considers the capitalist class of his own country, or many of its members, as traitors who have sold out to foreigners. In such conditions Marxism-as-analysis is inherently attractive: the analysis may not be right, but it is on the right side, which is more to the point.

Marxism-as-assurance, the predictive side, is even more attractive to Third World nationalists. If you have to fight against what appear to be overwhelming odds, it is good to know that the god of History is on your side, making eventual victory certain. Also, Marxism appeals to the universalist tendency present in all exalted nationalism. It offers an apparently secularized version of the old Puritan or Old Testament vision. History has singled out, let us say, the rebel nationalists of El Salvador to play a very special role in the salvation of the world. So Salvadorian nationalism gets holier and grander, rivaling, in its own way, that of the United States.

To the tidy-minded of the right, my view of these matters will appear absurdly fanciful. Marxists are Marxists, nationalists are nationalists, and never the twain shall meet. But they do meet, and can even merge. The United States got itself into deep trouble in Vietnam, through failing to recognize the presence of nationalists because they were talking Marxism. And those who are responsible for U.S. policy toward Central America today seem to have learned nothing from that costly lesson.

Third World Marxist nationalists generally do not regard Moscow as the infallible interpreter of Marxism. Carlos Fonseca, for example, founder of the Sandinista ideology, took no notice of a Moscow ruling that Nicaragua was unripe for revolution. Yet Third World Marxist nationalists may have no choice but to gravitate toward Moscow. Any Third World nationalist movement that uses Marxist language incurs the automatic hostility of Washington, soon brought to bear in modern versions of excommunication and interdict. Isolated and under pressure from the West, such movements are liable to become dependent on Moscow—Cuba and Nicaragua being the most obvious examples. And then of course the fact of the dependence can be used as an argument justifying the policies of isolation that produced the dependence in the first place.

The politics of the self-fulfilling prophecy have seldom been pursued with such consistency as in Washington's misguided efforts to contain Soviet power by punishing exponents of Marxist ideology. Through these efforts they have contrived to cast Moscow in the most attractive role available to it: defender of Third World nationalism.

Moscow has been somewhat hesitant about accepting that role, has sometimes refused it, and sometimes bungled it.

When Patrice Lumumba appealed for Soviet aid in 1961, he got just enough Soviet aid to ensure his own destruction at the hands of the CIA, aided by top officials of the United Nations. The Soviets were hardly inconsolable. The affair proved a propaganda bonanza for them throughout Africa. Its monument is the Patrice Lumumba University in Moscow.

Sometimes the Soviets have been handed great cards, courtesy of Uncle Sam, yet still managed to lose through their own unaided efforts. In the 1950s the fertile mind of John Foster Dulles, under the guidance of the Middle East experts of the British Foreign Office, dreamed up the Baghdad Pact. The Baghdad Pact was supposed to unite the Arab world in such a way as to exclude Soviet influence. Its immediate effect was to induce the most important Arab nationalist leader, Gamal Abdel Nasser, head of the most important Arab state, Egypt, to seek Soviet aid and get it. (A secondary effect was to destroy the only regime in the area that ever joined the Baghdad Pact, that in Baghdad itself.) This would later be depicted as a triumph for Soviet diplomacy. Actually it was a triumph, of a negative kind, for American and British diplomacy. But the Soviets were not sufficiently skillful to hold onto the present they had been handed. Nasser became disillusioned with them, and his successor, Anwar el-Sadat, ditched them altogether.

Soviet policy with regard to Third World nationalism has been marked, not by Machiavellian planning, but by half-hearted opportunism. The Horn of Africa provides good examples. There the Soviets began by supporting the Somali-nationalist and Marxist-speaking regime of Siad Barre. During this period those analysts who like to make our flesh creep about the long-range plans of the Kremlin's chess players had a field day by the Red Sea; there were little maps with arrows showing the pivotal importance of the Port of Berbera and the Straits of Bab al-Mandab. While the West had been asleep, the crafty Russians had secured possession of the geopolitical key to the most critical region in the world.

Then the same Russians, no doubt for some even craftier

reason, suddenly threw that key away. Following Colonel Mengistu's coup in Addis Ababa, the Soviets switched sides in the Ogaden War; Ethiopia, the enemy of their old client, became their new client. The Americans could have—and they now do have—Berbera and the Straits of Bab al-Mandab, and Colonel Barre and his Marxism. That had become the wrong kind of Marxism. The right kind of Marxism was that of Mengistu Haile Meriam, the Servant of Mary, and his Amharic cohorts in Addis Ababa.

Mengistu is not only a Marxist, he is also the Lion of Judah. To prove it he has a full-grown lion chained outside his office door. When I talked with Mengistu a few years ago, we could hear the lion coughing just outside the office; not roaring, just coughing, a dry melancholy cough that goes well with the tone and tenor of Colonel Mengistu's conversation.

As I left, I saw the lion, but was not allowed to photograph him. Apparently the lion might be confusing to Mengistu's international admirers, a progressive lot and rather literal-minded. The lion's message is strictly for the Ethiopians, to let them know where the sovereignty is: something they need to know.

Outside, in every street and square, are huge and rather beautiful pictures of Marx and Engels, with their hair and beards cut in the style of Coptic saints, and with the great round eyes of Ethiopian iconography.

The Siberian farmers of the Karl Marx Collective would feel quite at home with their Ethiopian comrades. Indeed some of the Old Bolshevik pioneers at the beginning of our century rallied behind their local equivalents of those Ethiopian ikons. The first Marxist May Day demonstration in the Caucasus took place in 1900, at a place called the Salt Lake, on the remote outskirts of Tiflis. The young ex-seminarian Josef Djugash-vili—who had yet to assume his underground name of Sta-lin—made his first public speech on this occasion. Stalin's biographer describes the scene: "The demonstrators closed their ranks and hoisted red banners. Home-made portraits of

Marx and Engels were raised aloft. The modest meeting was rather like an Orthodox religious procession with the icons, the holy pictures, replaced by the portraits of Marx and Engels."

I am not suggesting that the Soviets threw away their strategic prize on the Red Sea just to acquire one symbolic lion plus a complete set of Coptic ikons representing the founders of Marxism. No; I think the Soviets hightailed it into the highlands, not so much for the sake of what they might find there, as in order to get away from what they had.

What they had had was an embarrassing alliance with the hottest and holiest nationalism in all of black Africa. Somali nationalism is passionately irredentist. The country lays claim to all territories inhabited by Somalis. This means it wants to annex not just the Ethiopian Ogaden, but large chunks of Kenya, Sudan, and Djibouti. The claims are symbolized in Somalia's five-star flag. Pan-Somalian irredentism not only makes Somalia exceedingly unpopular in its own region, but makes it bad news throughout Africa. The principle it represents—revision of territorial boundaries in the light of tribal factors—threatens the very existence of virtually every other African state. So the Somali alliance did the Soviets no good in the rest of Africa. Worse than that, pan-Somali irredentism ran counter to the Soviet Union's most firmly held principle in international affairs. The Soviet Union is strongly opposed, for Chinese and other reasons, to all talk of boundary revision. Yet here they were stuck with the most manically irredentist bunch of nationalists currently at large anywhere in the world.

Apparently the Soviets originally had thought they could talk their Marxist friend Siad Barre out of his irredentist deviations. But as always nationalism proved stronger than Marxism. Siad Barre held fast to his five-star flag and his dream of Greater Somalia.

Mengistu's coup gave the Soviets an opportunity to extricate themselves, without too much loss of face, from their pan-Somalian imbroglio. They had lost one client, but they had acquired another. And at least their new friend, the Marxist Lion of Judah, was sound on irredentism. Ethiopia's boundaries, like those of the Soviet Union, were sacred.

Considerations of national prestige and the prestige of individuals connected to national prestige determine Soviet behavior in areas remote from its borders. (Security is the determinant in areas contiguous to its borders.) Its clients in distant regions—Cuba, Nicaragua, Angola, Ethiopia, Syria, South Yemen, Vietnam, North Korea—are often taken as evidence of a consistent "tomorrow the world" strategy. Perhaps so, but I doubt it. They look to me like a somewhat random and ramshackle clientele, acquired through accidents of history and liable to fall off through similar accidents, as Egypt, Somalia, and Mozambique have.

The main value to the Soviet Union of these clients is that they serve as status symbols. They mean that the Soviet Union has arrived as a global power, just like the United States. This flatters the nationalist feelings of the Soviet rulers and of Soviet citizens, and bonds them together. It also provides the national religion, Marxism, with enough apparent confirmation to shore up its shaky credibility.

If geopolitical strategy were the determinant, Somalia was surely the place to hold onto. But if status is the determinant, Ethiopia will do just as well.

The management of holy nationalism is the greatest problem in peacekeeping. Ideally those responsible for international affairs ought to be able to understand and moderate the holy nationalism of their own country and to discern, even when disguised, the operations and limits of holy nationalism in rival countries as well as in third-party countries.

Unfortunately this may be too much to hope for. There are serious cognitive difficulties involved. *Any* nationalism inherently finds it hard to understand any other nationalism or even to want to understand it. This is particularly true of holy nationalisms. Rejection of the other is part of the holiness.

Still, in the right circumstances, people can transcend these limitations, at least to some extent. There are some signs that circumstances today may be more propitious than they have been during the last six years. Gorbachev has shown a tendency to moderate some of the more obnoxious manifestations of Soviet holy nationalism. I do not believe that Ronald Reagan has any autonomous equivalent tendency. But the custodians whom he has been obliged to appoint, in place of the crusaders on whom he formerly relied, may represent such a tendency. And the same tendency may show itself in the choice of the next American president.

It may not be too much to hope that by the end of the next decade there could be a more stable accommodation between the superpowers, including a nuclear-test freeze, slowing down of the arms race, Soviet withdrawal from Afghanistan, and withdrawal of U.S. support for the Contras. In that more benign climate I would expect to see the return of the United States to acceptance of the jurisdiction of the World Court. Perhaps by 1990 the National Prayer Breakfast may be giving thanks for all that.

In terms of our tripartite scale of holy nationalism, I suggested that under the Reagan presidency the needle had come to hover ominously somewhere between "holy nation" and "deified nation." After November 1986 it dropped back to somewhere between "holy nation" and "chosen people." I would like to see the needle drop back, not a long way, but just a little farther.

It was Abraham Lincoln who spoke of the United States as "this almost chosen people." That "almost" is not the least precious part of your great heritage.

Notes
Index

Notes

1. Chosen Peoples, Promised Lands

1   the world." David Miller, ed., *The Blackwell Encyclopaedic of Political Thought* (Oxford: Basil Blackwell, 1986). The statement quoted is preceded by the words: "If an *ideology* is a general way of thinking about the world that has prescriptive implications for politics, then nationalism is an ideology and."

2   Rousseau. The earliest manifesto of cultural nationalism is probably Dante's *De Vulgari Eloquentia;* and the earliest manifesto of political nationalism, the Exhortation at the end of Machiavelli's *The Prince.* But these manifestos were not developed into full-blown ideologies.

4   (Luke 4:5–8). See also Matt. 8–10.

4   says Satan. In Luke. Matthew does not have these words.

5   Gentile enemies. For example, Gen. 22:17. W. M. Clark, "The Origin and Development of the Land Promise" (unpublished dissertation, Yale University), likens the God of the Old Testament to the War Gods of other ancient Middle Eastern cultures, and likens the covenant promises to War Oracles in those cultures.

6   precious faith." See Samuel Eliot Morison, *Builders of the Bay Colony* (Boston: New England University Press, 1982), p. 72. This is the same John Cotton who later, in the Bay Colony, persecuted and drove out Roger Williams, who *really* tried to do something for the Indians.

7   earthy religion." Rabbi Adin Steinsalz, at a *heder* conducted in English, which I attended, in Jerusalem. The *Encyclopaedia Judaica* defines *heder* as "the common name for the old-fashioned elementary school for the teaching of Judaism." The one I attended was on the level of a good graduate seminar, though no doubt it was elementary

in the sense of being an introduction to traditional Judaic thought. Most of the participants, I think, were Jews who had not received a religious education and had come to feel that they had missed something.

9   heathens from Africa.   The American Christian justification of the institution of slavery came to base itself in part on the theory that the blacks were the descendants of Ham, more specifically of his son Canaan, cursed by Noah and made servants to the descendants of Shem and Japheth. This seems to have been a rationalization succeeding the old "Africans are heathens."

9   purity of blood.   See Albert A. Sigroff, *Les Controverses des statuts de pureté de sang en Espagne du xvième au xviiième siècle* (Paris, 1960).

10   swinery."   Peter G. J. Pulzer, *The Rise of Political Anti-Semitism in Germany and Austria* (New York: Wiley, 1964).

10   "Gandhi's God"   *Religion* (January–February 1987).

12   monarchy of God."   Eusebius of Caesarea, "Tricennial Oration in Praise of Constantine," III. 5.

12   nature of the change   Some contemporaries also felt this way. "What has the Emperor to do with the Church?" inquired the fourth-century heresiarch Donatus. (For this and other references I am indebted to Steve Theodore, a student participant in my 1987 seminar on Religion and Nationalism at Williams College.)

12   quasi-Scriptural status.   See Domenico Comparetti, *Vergil in the Middle Ages*, trans. E. F. M. Benecke (London and New York, 1895).

13   city above."   Augustine *Contra Gaudentium* 1.37; quoted in Ernst Kantorowicz, *"Pro Patria Mori* in Mediaeval Thought," *American Historical Review* 56 (April 1951): 472–493.

15   by Christians.   Commenting on this paragraph, Owen Dudley Edwards writes: "One of the nice points about the erosion of celestial *patria* in the interests of terrestrial *patria,* is with relation to the Papal states themselves. By the time you get Pope Julius II that seems a good symbol of the transformation" (personal communication).

15   martyr of God."   Kantorowicz, *"Pro Patria Mori."* I am greatly indebted in this part of my chapter to this seminal paper.

16   Ghibellines."   *Inferno,* Canto x, line 120.

17   he who loses.)   *La Divina Commedia,* ed. H. Oelsner (London, 1935). English translation of Inferno by J. A. Carlyle.

17   against Jesus;   Only "very nearly," because Virgil points out that it is Judas who suffers most, *che ha maggior pena* (Canto xxxiv, line 61). Judas' head is inside Satan's mouth, while the legs of the other two are inside, their heads hanging out.

18 a cosmopolitan." Comparetti, *Vergil in the Middle Ages*, pp. 203–204.

19 future realities." Jacques Goudet, *Dante et la politique* (Paris, 1969), p. 229.

19 before our faces." The books of the Maccabees are classified as apocryphal in the Authorized Version, though ranking as canonical in the Douay Version, but 1 Macc., composed in Hebrew, is accepted as a genuine example of late Jewish religious nationalism in the line of the Old Testament.

20 The Empire is evil! Quoted in J. R. Strayer, *Mediaeval Statecraft and the Perspectives of History* (Princeton: Princeton University Press, 1971), p. 511.

20 religion of monarchy." "France, the Holy Land, the Chosen People and the Most Christian King," in Strayer, *Mediaeval Statecraft*, Princeton University Press, pp. 302, 314.

20 fabulous tales." Quoted in Auguste Vallet de Viriville, *Procès de condamnation de Jeanne D'Arc, dite la Pucelle d'Orléans* (Paris, 1867), p. 253.

21 Kingdom in trust." Quoted in Jules Michelet, *Histoire de France, Edition définitive*, 7 vols. (Paris, 1897), V, 51.

22 prescripts of the Church." Vallet de Viriville, *Procès*, p. 155.

22 Jeanne Darc was a saint." Michelet, *Histoire de France*, V, 157. The omission of "and" after "Religion" is interesting. "Religion and la Patrie" appear to be one.

2. New Chosen Peoples, New Promised Lands

23 Promised Land. Sebastian Brant, *The Ship of Fools* (1494). The passage, translated by E. H. Zeydel, is quoted in A. G. Dickens, *The German Nation and Martin Luther* (New York: Harper & Row, 1974), p. 26.

25 typology. Perry Miller's contention in *Roger Williams: His Contribution to the American Tradition* (Indianapolis: Bobbs-Merrill, 1953), pp. 34, 35, that "the great Protestant reformers" were "explicit in their condemnation of the typological method," has been shown to be an overstatement. See, e.g., Thomas M. Davis, "Traditions of Puritan Typology," in Sacvan Bercovitch, ed., *Typology and Early American Literature* (Amherst: University of Massachusetts Press, 1971).

26 from God." secrets!" and for Him." *The Writings and Speeches of Oliver Cromwell*, ed. Wilbur Cortez Abbott, 4 vols. (Cambridge,

Mass.: Harvard University Press, 1937; New York: Russell & Russell, 1970), III, 579; IV, 445; III, 60–61.

27 all Europe?" John Milton, *Areopagitica* (1644).

27 Hugh Seton-Watson, *Nations and States: An Enquiry into the Origins of Nations and the Politics of Nationalism* (Boulder, Colo.: Westview, 1977), p. 34.

28 outward objects." William Bradford, *History of Plymouth Plantation* (Boston, 1856), chap. 9.

28 geography." Robert Middlekauff, *The Mathers: Three Generations of Puritan Intellectuals, 1596–1728* (New York: Oxford University Press, 1971), p. 62.

29 hath been?" dismal example." Ibid., pp. 101, 103.

29 prevail." Quoted in Winthrop S. Hudson, ed., *Nationalism and Religion in America: Concepts of American Identity and Mission* (New York: Harper & Row, 1970), p. 28.

30 animates my lay. Quoted in Ernest Lee Tuveson, *Redeemer Nation: The Idea of America's Millennial Role* (Chicago: University of Chicago Press, 1968), p. 106.

30 covenant with God." Summarized in Middlekauff, *The Mathers,* p. 138.

31 Faith?" National Religion." *The Complete Writings of Roger Williams,* ed. Perry Miller, 7 vols. (New York: Russell & Russell, 1963), II, 264; IV, 442.

32 Leopard spots." God-pleasure, etc." themselves!" Quoted in James Ernst, *Roger Williams: New England Firebrand* (New York: AMS Press, 1932), pp. 95, 459, 106.

32 God Land," *Complete Writings,* VI, 319.

34 people of the dream. Timothy Smith, "Religion and Ethnicity in America," *American Historical Review* 83 (December 1978): 1155–1185. See also Werner Sollors, *Beyond Ethnicity: Consent and Descent in American Culture* (New York: Oxford University Press, 1986), for a subtle and resourceful exploration of immigrant culture; chap. 2, "Typology and Ethnogenesis," is especially relevant.

36 Catholics. Father Charles E. Coughlin, the "radio priest" of the 1930s, a precursor of McCarthy, appealed to the same kinds of audience. But Coughlin may reasonably be classed as a commentator, rather than a politician.

37 what God hath wrought. See Donald F. Crosby, S.J., *God, Church and Flag: Senator Joseph R. McCarthy and the Catholic Church, 1950–1957* (Chapel Hill: University of North Carolina Press, 1978).

38 machinery." *Harper's Magazine* 14 (June–November 1858): 694–

700. This final passage is not among those cited by Tuveson in *Redeemer Nation.*

38 Paul D. Escott, *After Secession: Jefferson Davis and the Failure of Confederate Nationalism* (Baton Rouge: Louisiana State University Press, 1978).

39 Dáil Eireann.   Lower, or popularly elected, branch of the Irish Parliament; analogous to the House of Commons.

42 chosen people with tenure   For that happy academic formula I am indebted to Professor Paul Dolan of the State University of New York at Stony Brook.

3. Puritanism, Enlightenment, Nationalism

43 Country."   Lester J. Cappon, ed., *The Adams-Jefferson Letters* (Chapel Hill: University of North Carolina Press, 1959), II, 525.

44 Jansenism among them."   Cotton Mather, *Magnalia Christi Americana* (1702; Hartford: Silas Andrus & Son, 1853), I, 249.

49 choose them afresh."   survive."   Spinoza, *Tractatus Theologico-Politicus* (1670). See *Benedict de Spinoza: The Political Works,* ed. A. G. Wernham (Oxford: Clarenden, 1958).

50 liberty."   Quoted in Ernest Hamel, *Histoire de Robespierre,* 3 vols. (Paris, 1865–1866), II, 171.

50 left there."   Jules Michelet, *Journal,* 7 August 1831. I am indebted for this important reference to Susan Dunn, Professor of French at Williams College.

51 world."   Quoted in R. R. Ergang, *Herder and the Foundations of German Nationalism* (New York, 1931), p. 71. Ergang, paraphrasing large tracts of Herder, provides a fine example of the compulsive usage of the adjective "national" by nationalists: "The individual prophets, writers, artists or poets are but the means employed by the national soul to give expression to a national religion, a national language or a national literature. They are those of the national group who are most responsive to the stimuli sent out by the national mind" (p. 87).

53 Millennial State."   For general background, see Alan Heimert's pioneering and comprehensive *Religion and the American Mind: From the Great Awakening to the Revolution* (Cambridge, Mass.: Harvard University Press, 1966). See also Sacvan Bercovitch, "The Typology of America's Mission," *American Quarterly* 30 (Summer 1978): 135–155, who quotes a number of contemporary sermons in this sense.

55 schism shops."   John Adams, *The Works of John Adams,* ed. Charles Francis Adams, 10 vols. (Boston, 1850–1856), X, 288. Similarly,

Jonathan Mayhew argues, in his Dudleian Lecture at Harvard in 1765, that "our controversy with Rome is not merely a religious one." It involved, according to Mayhew, "a defense of our laws, liberty and civil rights as men." Quoted in Pauline Maier, "The Pope at Harvard: The Dudleian Lectures; Anti-Catholicism and the Politics of Protestantism," *Proceedings of the Massachusetts Historical Society* 97 (1985): 16–41.

55 Carl Bridenbaugh, *Mitre and Sceptre: Transatlantic Faiths, Ideas, Personalities and Politics, 1689–1775* (New York: Oxford University Press, 1962), p. 260.

55 vitality." Heimert, *Religion and the American Mind*, p. 354.

58 two peoples. Charles H. Metzger, S.J., *The Quebec Act* (New York: United States Catholic Historical Society, 1936), pp. 152–153.

59 effigy of the Pope." Edward Frank Humphrey, *Nationalism and Religion in America, 1774–1789* (Boston: Chapman Law Publishing Company, 1924), p. 127.

59 Spain. The Revolutionaries unsuccessfully sought direct alliance with Spain. His Most Catholic Majesty showed more concern for ideological consistency than did either the Revolutionaries or His Most Christian Majesty.

61 OBEDIENCE TO GOD. by night." Report on a Seal for the United States, with Related Papers (20 August 1776), in Julian P. Boyd, ed., *The Papers of Thomas Jefferson* (Princeton: Princeton University Press, 1950), I, 494–495. Jefferson's design showed on the reverse "HENGIST AND HORSA, the Saxon chiefs from whom we claim the honour of being descended, and whose political principles we have assumed." I am indebted for this reference to Professor Jere P. Daniell of Dartmouth College.

62 American cause." *Encyclopedia Americana*, art, "Great Seal."

4. God Land Now

67 "friendship in Christ." It is only fair to add that in spirit the National Prayer Breakfasts appear to be ecumenical as regards inter-Christian relations; and they exhibit a rather vague benevolence toward other religions. Anti-Semitism is condemned. So is racism; Coretta King presented a New Testament reading at the 1987 National Prayer Breakfast. Yet the fact that these breakfasts, regularly attended by the highest constitutional officers, are exclusively Christian in character must be a little disturbing to the millions of Americans who are not Christians. Hence, perhaps, some of the awkward silences.

68 installments." A strong military emphasis seems to be a constant feature of the National Prayer Breakfast. At the 35th Annual NPB, February 5, 1987, the opening prayer was delivered by Admiral Carlyle A. H. Trost, Chief of Naval Operations. It was preceded by a musical selection, "There Is a Balm in Gilead," performed by the U.S. Naval Academy Chapel Choir. After "Balm in Gilead" the chairman of the 1987 NPB, Representative Daniel Coats, introduced Admiral Trost with the words: "Ladies and Gentlemen, few know of the wonderful fellowship that exists among the chiefs of our armed forces. Prayer plays a very real part in the lives of these men."

Also, although these proceedings are informal enough to elude the attention of most American civilians, they are broadcast to the armed forces. As Coats put it: "We are also joined today by members of our armed forces nationwide and worldwide through the Armed Forces Communications Network." *Congressional Record,* 100th Cong., 1st sess., 1987, Vol. 133, pt. 34. This is based on a text supplied by Congressman Coats, who described it as "a transcript"; I do not know whether or not it was edited. If not, the proceedings of the 35th NPB were less enlivening than those of the one I attended.

68 screen of all." Garry Wills, *Reagan's America: Innocents at Home* (New York: Doubleday, 1987), p. 361.

69 better than nothing. *Some* contemporary American religious teachers—e.g., the Reverend Jerry Falwell and his Liberation Front—far from inhibiting ultranationalism, actively encourage and excite it. But this is only one tendency, even among fundamentalists.

73 fishing season starts. Caroline Humphrey, *Karl Marx Collective: Economy, Society, and Religion in a Siberian Collective Farm* (New York: Cambridge University Press, 1983), p. 408.

74 helps Soviet power. From a 1965 paper, "On the Contemporary Situation of Shamanism in Siberia," quoted in Humphrey, *Karl Marx Collective,* p. 414. Soviet ethnographers are required to discuss such phenomena in the context of the need to "overcome survivals" of Shamanism, Lamaism, etc. But there does not seem to be an ugly rush to overcome a form of "survival," such as that of the Parisian communards, which "helps Soviet power."

78 need to know. Emperor Haile Selassie used the title "Lion of Judah" and kept a live lion to make the point. Mengistu, who is widely believed to have killed Haile Selassie, drops the title but keeps the lion.

79 Engels." Isaac Deutscher, *Stalin: A Political Biography,* rev. ed. (London: Penguin, 1966; repr. 1976), p. 54.

Index